Culinary Arts Institute

WINE

in Cooking and Dining

Featured in cover photo:
Beef Burgundy, page 52

WINE

WINE IN COOKING AND DINING

**Barbara MacDonald
and the Culinary Arts Institute Staff:**

Helen Geist: Director
Sherrill Corley: Editor • Ethel La Roche: Editorial Assistant
Ivanka Simatic: Recipe Tester
Edward Finnegan: Executive Editor • Patricia Westphal: Copy Editor
Charles Bozett: Art Director • John Mahalek: Art Assembly

Book designed and coordinated by Charles Bozett and Laurel DiGangi

Illustrations by David Cunningham

Adventures in Cooking SERIES

in Cooking and Dining

Culinary Arts Institute®
A DIVISION OF DELAIR PUBLISHING COMPANY.

FOREWORD

"What wine should we serve?" "Which wines can be used for cooking?" Worries about wine can plague a host and hostess and spoil the fun of a party—before it ever takes place!

Yet in countries where wine is everyday fare, people use it with no more concern than Americans give soft drinks. Wine is accepted and expected; it adds enjoyment, not constraints.

The history book helps to explain why Americans are just now getting acquainted with wine.

In colonial days, very little European wine was shipped here, and the price of the wine that was smuggled in was really a crime! The native American grapes just didn't make wine like that from European grapes. The colonists who planned ahead and brought *Vitis vinifera* (vines from European vineyards) with them found the New England soil an unfriendly host.

Vitis vinifera did better in California; by the late 1700s they had a good roothold there. But history had more headaches in store. Phylloxera, a louse deadly to *Vitis vinifera* roots, struck the California vineyards in the 1890s. It had already ravaged European vineyards, having traveled there on some native American vines. The cure in California, as in Europe, was to graft *Vitis vinifera* vines onto phylloxera-resistant native American roots.

The Temperance Movement, which ultimately led to Prohibition, was the next roadblock. In 1920, the new wine industry found itself outside the law. The vineyards that had just been reestablished were now illegal. Even after Prohibition was repealed, it took years to restore the vineyards to productivity. But since World War II, things have looked up for wine in America. It has been perfected to the point where it commands worldwide respect, and only a few countries lead us in production.

Still, the wine bottle is not quite at home on the American table. Perhaps that's because of a certain mystique that has grown up around wine service. Rather than risk serving the wrong wine before dinner, many hosts play it safe and serve the old familiar cocktails.

And, unlike skills that have passed from one generation to the next, wine seasoning is something that today's cooks must pick up on their own. Good food and good wine are both available; the ingredient too often lacking is confidence.

For the beginner, this book is planned to provide that confidence. It also offers serving and cooking suggestions for those whose friendship with wine is fully aged.

Copyright © 1976 by
Delair Publishing Company, Inc.
420 Lexington Avenue,
New York, New York 10170

ISBN: 0-8326-0548-4
Library of Congress Catalog Card
Number: 75-27332

ACKNOWLEDGMENTS

Advisory Council for Jams, Jellies and Preserves; American Lamb Council;
California Avocado Advisory Board; California Wine Advisory Board;
Rice Council for Market Development; Richard A. Schoch, Korbel Wineries;
Schaefer's Wines and Liquors, Skokie, Illinois; Washington Apple Commission

CONTENTS

MEET THE MANY KINDS OF WINE

"Cooking without wine is to run the gamut of flavor from A to C," asserts the continental chef, with a sly wink.

He's only half kidding. He really believes that the complete flavor alphabet can only be experienced through employing the artistry of wine. He believes, too, that wine served as aperitif prepares the palate for an extraordinary dining experience. Wine used in dishes to add subtle flavor shading and served with the meal brings the promise to fulfillment.

WHAT IS WINE?

Wine is generally understood to mean the fermented juice of grapes, although wine can be made from other plant juices. Wine is truly a "natural food" as it will develop on its own wherever sweet plant juices are allowed to collect and ferment.

But man has learned to help the process along through viticulture (the science of growing and harvesting the grapes) and viniculture (the art of making the wine). What he has developed is not one simple beverage, but a whole array. It helps the wine shopper to know that all wines fall into a few categories: appetizer and dessert wines, red and white table wines, and sparkling wines. To see how individual wines fit into the grouping, see the chart on page 9.

When it comes time for you to make that critical decision about which wine to buy, consider the use you'll make of it. Do you want something pleasant to serve with appetizers before dinner, or is the call for something to sip along with late evening conversation? In the first case, select an appetizer wine; in the second, a dessert wine.

APPETIZER AND DESSERT WINES

APPETIZER WINES

Sometimes appetizer wines and dessert wines are grouped separately, but since there are similarities between the two, it is simpler to consider them as one class. Appetizer and dessert wines generally have a higher alcoholic content and a more pronounced flavor than other wines.

In some cases, appetizer and dessert wines are the same wine in a different form. Take sherry and port. These wines are as much at home as aperitif as with dessert. The difference is in the dryness of the wine. "Dry" versions (with an absence of sweetness) are served for aperitif, and sweeter forms for dessert. The exception to this rule is vermouth, which is popular in both its dry and sweet forms for the before-dinner hour. Someone discovered that sweet vermouth (the Italian version) mixed with whiskey, makes an agreeable cocktail, and the Manhattan has been a fixture ever since. Dry vermouth (the French version) makes a dandy cocktail, too, as every Martini mixer knows. In some classifications, vermouth shows up as an "aromatized" wine, as it is flavored with herbs, spices, and peels.

Since most wine rules are flexible, there is nothing wrong with pouring a little of the wine slated to accompany the meal to sip during the pre-dinner hour. For everyday meals, this is probably the practice in most homes. But sherry, port, and vermouth all keep well when tightly closed and refrigerated, so it's not extravagant to keep an appetizer wine on hand for family meals.

DESSERT WINES

Like dessert itself, dessert wines should be sweet and full-bodied. In addition to sweet (or "cream") sherry, there are several other distinct types, including the muscat wines, port, tokay, French Sauternes, and sweet semillon.

Of the wines made from muscat grapes, muscatel is perhaps the best known in this country.

Port is one name applied to several wines—all guaranteed to take the edge off any storm! The original is made in Portugal, and the legal definition there of port is "wine which has been shipped over the bar of Oporto." Now, Portuguese port is called "Porto" in this country, to distinguish it from American ports.

Red port is rich and fruity. Tawny port claims the highest respect and a price to match; it has spent more time in oak casks and is more mature. White port (which is really straw colored) is not as toney as tawny, but has its fans, nonetheless.

Amber-colored California tokay has a flavor that lies somewhere between a port and sherry. All true Tokay comes from a district in Hungary; its Hungarian name is Tokaj.

French Sauternes is a sweet wine, quite different from the dry white American wines called "sauterne" (without the final *s*). Sauternes is a district of the Bordeaux region. The fragrant, golden-colored sweet wine produced there is the real Sauternes, a perfect dessert accompaniment.

Sweet semillon is the American adaptation of the French Sauternes. The label "haut sauterne" on a California wine usually means that the wine is semisweet.

In addition to these wines, you are apt to find special natural wines, such as apple, cherry, and grape wines with fruit flavors in the wine shop. These are classed as dessert wines.

"Kosher" wines refer to any wine certified by a rabbi. The largest production is of a very sweet red kosher wine made mainly from Concord grapes in eastern states where the addition of sugar is permitted.

TABLE WINES

To belong in this category, a wine must be compatible with other flavors. Whereas aperitif and dessert wines are more assertive, table wines are good harmonizers. They are also dry. All dinner wines, red, rosé, and white, average 12½ percent alcohol.

RED TABLE WINES

If you're shopping for wine to serve with the meal, let your menu be your guide. In "Ways with Wine" (page 22), you'll find the familiar advice "red wine with red meat and white wine with white meat." This has become tradition because it seems to work so well. Full-bodied red wine is robust; so is red meat.

Such a wine might overpower a more delicate meat such as veal or turkey, to which a lighter wine is better suited.

Supposing rib roast is on the menu. From the red table wines, consider burgundy, pinot noir, vino rosso, or any of those listed except rosé. Rosé is included with the red wines as even a trace of red takes a wine out of the "white" category. Despite claims that "rosé goes with everything," it would be unsuited to roast beef or steaks.

Rosé does have its place; it's pleasant with luncheon foods or on a picnic. And it is sometimes the choice when serving ham, which is neither red nor white meat.

WHITE TABLE WINES

When chicken, fish, veal, or any light meat holds star billing on your menu, a white table wine belongs in the supporting cast. Excellent domestic and foreign wines are available in all categories.

Among the domestic selections, you'll find California chablis, ranging from medium to very dry, and pale golden in color. California rhine wine is usually a bit more tart and lighter in color. Domestic sauterne varies from dry to sweet, depending upon brand. See the wine classification chart on page 9 for the European counterparts, and experiment with foreign as well as American-made wines.

Table wines that are suitable for everyday use can be purchased in "jugs" (half-gallons or gallons) at a budget price.

SPARKLING WINES

Champagne and sparkling burgundy are two of the most popular sparkling wines. Champagne is so versatile that it can be served with any course of the meal, or accompany cocktail food at a party. Sparkling burgundy is sweeter; it works best as a dessert wine.

The effervescence of the best sparkling wines is brought about by a second fermentation in closed containers. Their alcoholic content, like the still dinner wines, averages 12½ percent.

In France, Champagne can only be produced within a legally defined area which was formerly called Champagne. In some other countries, including our own, the name has become attached to a white sparkling wine produced by the champagne process or a variation of it.

WINE NAMES

The names that identify the wines that fit into the classifications described above are many. If you like memory aids, you can further classify wine names into groupings of generic, varietal, proprietary, and color names.

WINE CLASSIFICATIONS

Here are a few examples of the various classes; not an all-inclusive list, but a basic outline for a closer acquaintance with wine.

American Wines	European Wines To Which Related
APPETIZER WINES	
Sherry (dry)	Jerez (fino) (Spanish)
Vermouth (dry)	Vermouth (French)
Vermouth (sweet)	Vermouth (Italian)
Port (white)	Porto (white) (Portuguese)
Dubonnet (red and blonde)	Dubonnet (French)
DESSERT WINES	
Sherry (sweet or cream)	Jerez (oloroso) (Spanish)
Muscatel	Muscat doré de Frontignan (French), Muscat de Samos (Greek), Moscato (Italian), Moscatel (Portuguese), and others
Port (Ruby and Tawny)	Porto (Ruby and Tawny) (Portuguese)
Tokay	Tokay (Hungarian)
RED TABLE WINES	
Pinot Noir, Petite Sirah	Red Burgundy Wines (French)
Cabernet Sauvignon, Claret	Red Bordeaux Wines (French)
Gamay Beaujolais	Beaujolais (French)
Barbera	Barbera (Italian)
Chianti	Chianti, Chianti Classico (Italian)
Grignolino	Grignolino (Italian)
Rosé, Gamay Rosé, Grenache Rosé, and others	Tavel Rosé (and others, French), Rosato (Italian), Roditys (Greek), and others
Zinfandel (exclusively Californian)	
WHITE TABLE WINES	
Pinot Chardonnay, Chablis	White Burgundy Wines (French)
Sauvignon Blanc	White Bordeaux Wines (French)
Chenin Blanc	Vouvray (Loire Valley, French)
Semillon	White Graves (French)
Johannisberg Riesling	Rhine Wines and Moselle Wines (German)
Sylvaner	Sylvaner (German)
Gewürztraminer	Gewürztraminer (Alsatian)
SPARKLING WINES	
Champagne	Champagne (French), Asti Spumante (Italian), Sekt (German), and others
Sparkling Burgundy	Sparkling Burgundy (French)

GENERIC NAMES

These names have geographic origins. Rhine wine originally came from the valley of the Rhine River in Germany; Champagne and Burgundy (and many others) from France. American made wines bearing such names are usually similar to the originals. In some cases, giving a wine a geographic name is a little like calling a cheese "Swiss" or a pastry "French" if it is made in a certain way, regardless of where it is made. A problem enters the picture when an imitator capitalizes on a famous name for a wine that resembles the original loosely, if at all.

Other geographic distinctions are found on American labels which state, for example, "California Burgundy," or "New York State Champagne." Some labels now state "American," an indication that not all of the wine in the bottle is from one state. One New York winemaker now bottles "American Chablis." Most of this wine is from California, blended and bottled in New York State.

VARIETAL NAMES

A wine named for the grape that supplies the major portion of the juice going into its production has a "varietal" name.

California law requires that at least 51 percent of the juice in a wine must come from the named variety of grape. Many wines contain a higher percentage, and some contain 100 percent of the named grape.

Other countries have their own laws about varietal names. Very often 100 percent of the named grape must be used.

One example of a varietal-named California wine is Pinot Noir. This tells the buyer something about the composition of the wine, and is preferred by many to wine sold under the simpler generic name of Burgundy.

Another example is California Pinot Chardonnay, which bears a close resemblance to the French Chablis and is made from the same grape which has been transplanted here. Johannisberg Riesling has the same relationship to most German Rhine wine, because much of the Rhine wine is made from Riesling grapes.

PROPRIETARY NAMES

Occasionally a winemaker will decide to give a wine a name that does not conform to other classifications. He may, in fact, coin a name, just as brand names are given to other products. Very often advertising campaigns are constructed to establish and promote such names, in the hope of winning return customers.

COLOR NAMES

While this system applies more to the unpretentious than to the great wines, table wines are often referred to simply as "red," "white," or "pink" (or rosé, as the French would say).

As careful observers know, these names cover a far wider range of color than single hues. "Red" includes everything from the nearly black to light crimson. And some of the darker pinks are nearly red. The Greek "roditis" (pink), for example, is nearly as dark as some reds.

And "white," while never chalky white, can be nearly as crystal-clear as water. Or it may be as dark as amber, or a shade in between.

Wine color is not always determined by grape color. The length of time that the grape skins are left in the "must" (grape juice before it is fermented) plays a far more critical role. If they are removed immediately after the grapes are crushed, white wine results. If they remain about a day, the wine is pink. Longer contact produces red wine.

Rosé shares some qualities with both red and white wines, but the finer rosés are not a blend of the two. Rosé is made from black grapes alone. The wine is not fermented entirely with the grape skins, as are red wines, nor completely without, as are white wines. The skins are removed when the desired color is reached.

American "red," "white," and "rosé" table wines are often the domestic counterparts of the French *vin ordinaire* and the Italian *vino de tavola*, everyday table wines.

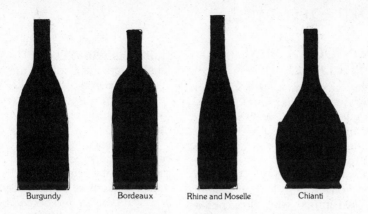

Burgundy   Bordeaux   Rhine and Moselle   Chianti

WHAT THE BOTTLE TELLS YOU

A visit to a wine shop can be a little overwhelming; in addition to a multitude of American wines, you'll find many with labels from all over the world! If there is a salesperson standing by, feel free to ask him questions. It's the second best way to learn. The best, of course, is to sample the wine itself.

But suppose you're on your own, faced by a strange bottle of wine. What does the exterior tell you about the contents? A lot, if you can read the clues.

BOTTLE SHAPE AND COLOR

WIDE AND GENTLY SLOPING TO A SLENDER NECK

The wines of Burgundy come in bottles of this shape. Bottles holding red Burgundy wines are dark green in color. Light-colored glass so fashioned hold French white burgundies, such as Chablis and American white burgundies. The Champagne bottle is of this general shape, though wider and heavier, to withstand the pressure from the bubbles inside. The Champagne bottle is green.

STRAIGHT SIDES WITH "SHOULDERS"

This is the classic Bordeaux bottle. French Bordeaux and the American claret counterparts come in this bottle. Like the Burgundies, red wines come in green bottles, and white wines in light-colored bottles.

TALL AND GENTLY SLOPING BOTTLES

This is the traditional bottle of the German Moselles and Rhine wines. California Rieslings come in green bottles of the same shape; Rhine and Rhine-type wines usually are in brown.

ROUND BOTTLES WRAPPED IN RAFFIA

These hold some Italian and California chiantis.

UNUSUAL SHAPES

Flasks with unusual shapes have been designed by some wine bottlers to attract attention. One California producer puts his highest-quality port and sherry into heart-shaped bottles. A well-known rosé, formerly marketed in a pottery jug, is now found in insulated glass fashioned in the same jug shape. There is no one distinctively shaped bottle for rosé; it can be found in bottles of many different shapes.

CORKS

Some say the cork in a wine bottle is merely a status symbol. Does it tell you anything about the wine in the bottle? The answer is "yes," if the cork is there because the wine is the sort that needs aging. Most of the world's finest wines do benefit from aging, and corks play an important role in the process. But since most of the wine that is made is meant to be consumed as soon as it is bottled, the cork is unnecessary in most cases.

Plastic corks are often found in bottles of sparkling wines. Domestic sherry and port usually come with a screw-type top. And many inexpensive table wines have a simple closure that doesn't need a corkscrew.

But for the fine red and white wines that do need aging, cork permits the slow evaporation and gradual oxidation that gives rise to bouquet. Many vintners perforate the colored capsule outside the cork to allow exposure to air.

A cork's length should be in proportion to the aging period of the wine. A great Bordeaux will need a longer cork than a Beaujolais, for example. So that the cork won't dry out and let in too much air, store a corked bottle on its side.

YOU CAN JUDGE A WINE
BY ITS LABEL

The label is the winemaker's message to you about his wine. Foreign labels usually offer enough information in English to guide the American shopper, but the terminology can be confusing. And the requirements for what must appear on the label vary from country to country.

This section opens with a look at the American label. It is followed by notes on labels from several countries from which we import wine. It is not a complete coverage of the world's wine-producing countries, but it features a few whose wines and cuisines have had a strong influence on our own.

AMERICAN WINES

Most of the wine Americans buy is American, and most of that, from California.

California Wines: The history of California winemaking is peopled with explorers, priests, and entrepreneurs. Cortez, the Spanish conqueror, made the first impact in 1524 by ordaining that winemaking would be one of the industries of the New World.

Priests in the early California missions were among the first vintners. Father Juan Ugarte made plantings in lower California in 1697, and other missions helped the new industry to flourish. When the Mexican government secularized the missions in the 1830s, their vineyards were abandoned.

By the 1850s, private vineyards had taken their place, and in 1851, Count Haraszthy, a colorful Hungarian nobleman, introduced a number of European varietals of the *Vitis vinifera* to California soil. These included the Zinfandel vines which have produced one of the state's most popular red wines. The Count experimented in various regions of the state to see which vines grew best where.

California Wine-Producing Areas: California wine country can be divided into three areas: the North Coast counties centered around San Francisco; the interior valleys, running from Sacramento in the north to Kern County in the south; and the South Coast region, which includes the San Fernando Valley and all of San Bernardino County.

The North Coast counties are credited with producing California's best dry table wines.

Considered to be the most important development in the production of California wine is the effort to improve the quality of varietal wines, those named for the grape variety such as Riesling and Pinot Noir. Many observers feel that American wines will increase their potential to compete with European wines as the quantity and quality of these varietals grow.

California Wine Labels: The state law requires that label statements conform to these rules:

1. The name of the maker must be shown.

2. If a vintage year is shown (it's not, usually) all of the wine in the bottle must have been produced in that year.

3. The origin cannot be identified unless 75 percent of the wine comes from grapes grown and fermented in the region named.

4. A statement of alcoholic content is required.

5. "Produced and bottled by" means that at least 75 percent of the wine was crushed, matured, and bottled by the named vintner. If in place of "produced and bottled by" you find the word "made," as much as 90 percent of the wine may have been produced by others. But if "estate bottled" appears on the label, 100 percent of the wine has been made by the estate.

6. The type of wine must be shown on the label. This may be a generic, varietal, or proprietary name. For a listing of some California varietals and their relationship to their European counterparts, see the chart on page 9.

Other Western Wines: The states of Washington, Oregon, and Arizona are capable of growing *Vitis vinifera* grapes, and therefore of producing wines similar to the European greats. Such wines are now being made, and the future looks promising. Washington's bay area at Puget Sound also grows native grapes, and produces wine similar to that from the eastern states.

Other American or Eastern Wines: To call wine produced east of the West Coast "Eastern" sounds like a misnomer, but in practice, that often happens. The name has more to do with grape variety than geography.

Conditions favor growing *Vitis vinifera* varietals in the far west, but native vines do better elsewhere. Some *Vitis vinifera* are grown in the midwest and scattered points east, but the Concord grape, a member of the *Vitis labrusca*, is more widely planted. This is the same blue-black grape used by your grandmother (and now perhaps, you!) to make jelly. Juice from this grape is used in kosher wines.

Perhaps you've heard the term "foxy" applied to wine; it describes the distinctive flavor of *Vitis labrusca* wines. To fanciers of European and California wines, the foxy flavor is objectionable. But the high sales of kosher wine show it has fans, too.

Experimentation with crossing European and native vines has brought good results. So has blending wine from California with eastern wines.

American Wine Producing Areas: State law determines where wine can be made, and, of course, soil and climate play deciding roles. Where permit-

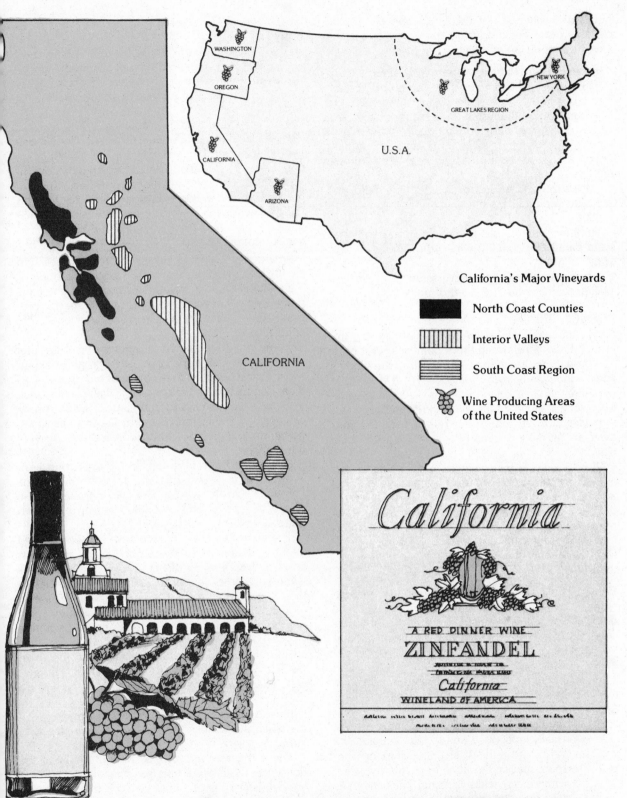

WASHINGTON

OREGON

CALIFORNIA

ARIZONA

NEW YORK

GREAT LAKES REGION

U.S.A.

California's Major Vineyards

North Coast Counties

Interior Valleys

South Coast Region

Wine Producing Areas
of the United States

CALIFORNIA

California

A RED DINNER WINE

ZINFANDEL

California

WINELAND OF AMERICA

American Wines

ted, small wineries dot the landscape across the country, but major producing areas are states in the Great Lakes region and New York State.

American Wine Labels: Some federal regulations apply to all American wine. The Bureau of Alcohol, Tobacco, and Firearms, in cooperation with the Food and Drug Administration, is responsible for enforcing them. As with food products, standards of identity have been set for wine names. Government approval is needed to insure that wine names comply with these standards.

Labels must show alcoholic content, quantity, and the name and address of the importer, producer, or bottler.

Another federal rule requires "American" in a wine name that contains wine from more than one state.

Aside from these regulations, some states, such as California, have their own set of rules.

FRENCH WINES

Eating and drinking are necessities of life, but the French have transformed them both into art forms.

Although it is recognized that much of the world's finest wine comes from France, it is also a fact that most French wine is *vin ordinaire*—everyday wine. Such labels as *vin rouge, vin blanc,* and *vin rosé,* signifying nothing more than red, white, and rosé wine, are far more common than the wines with lofty titles.

Wine is to the French what tea is to the English; it is as common on the French table as milk or soft drinks are on ours.

Of the ninety departments in France, about two-thirds have commercial vineyards. The most important wine-producing districts are Champagne, Alsace, Burgundy, the Rhone Valley, Bordeaux, and the Loire Valley.

French Wine Labels: Once a wine has attained fame, what is to keep an imitator from copying the name as well as the product? To cope with this question, and to assure the buyer that he is getting what he bargains for, the French have set up rigid requirements for their wine labels.

In 1935 the French established standards for over two hundred different wines. As a result, the term *Appellation Contrôlée* appears on some French wine labels. Translated, it means that the name on the label is officially recognized and legally defined. The wine must come from the district, township, or vineyard (the more specific the label, the better the wine, usually!) from which it takes its name. The wine must be produced from certain established varieties of grapes and no others, and from grapes that have achieved a specified minimum of ripeness. It must

have been made according to the traditions of its district.

The term *Appellation Contrôlée* has nothing to do with quality. In other words, it is no promise of goodness, but it does assure the buyer of origin, grape variety, ripeness, and methods used in making the wine.

You may also find the notation *V.D.Q.S. (vins délimités de qualité supérieure).* These include many fine wines which happen not to qualify for *Appellation Contrôlée.* Nevertheless, the French government strictly controls their production zone, variety of grape, and yield per acre. If, along with *V.D.Q.S.* you find the words *label de Garantie* you will know that the wine has been tasted and approved by a committee of impartial experts.

Champagne does not carry the term *Appellation Contrôlée* but in the case of the French Champagne, the name itself is your assurance that what you have purchased is a specific wine, made by a specific process, from certain varieties of grape, in a legally defined area of France.

Some countries have trade agreements stating that Champagne is an appellation of origin and belongs to the French alone. These countries have developed their own names for their sparkling white wines (such as Sekt in Germany, and Spumante in Italy). American vintners are not prevented by law from using the name, and some have produced excellent copies of the French.

Cru is another notation sometimes found on French wines, and literally translated, means "growth." On the label it generally indicates a wine of special quality, and probably wears a pricetag to match.

The wine districts of France have all been divided into better and not-quite-so-good areas at various times. In 1855, in Bordeaux, a list of the best wines were assigned orders of quality; the five top classes then assigned were the five *crus classé* or classified growths. These classifications still appear; they apply only to wines of the Médoc area, and in a separate classification, to those of Sauternes.

But *cru* may be found on wines from the other districts of France, such as the *premier cru* Burgundies. These are special occasion wines for most of us, as the price discourages everyday use.

French wines may show alcoholic content, but if the label says simply "table wine," it averages 12½ percent.

The shipper or importer is shown, usually at the bottom of the label. If you find one whose products are consistently good, it will pay you to return to his wine.

The vintage year may be shown on the label or on a separate neck label. These dates can be your guide

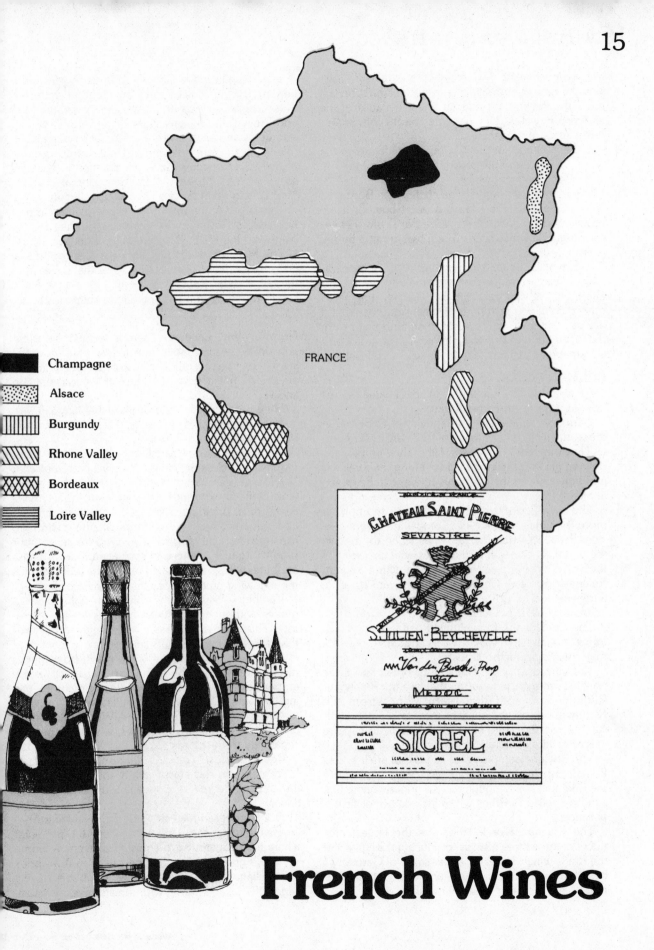

Champagne

Alsace

Burgundy

Rhone Valley

Bordeaux

Loire Valley

FRANCE

French Wines

to how much aging a wine needs, but dates for individual wines require a little extra study. Hard and fast rules about aging are difficult to set because of the variation in wines. The wine merchant is often your best source of guidance.

Some regions, such as Champagne, date only the wines of exceptional years; the dated wines are known as "vintage" wines.

Mis (or *mise*) *en bouteille au chateau* on Bordeaux wine means that the wine has been bottled at the property where it was made. *Mise par le propriétaire* on Burgundy wine means that it was bottled by the grower.

The whole subject of French wine is quite complex. It was in France that wine-making reached its apex, and its wines remain the basis for judging all others. So if you're serious in your study of wine, it will pay you to do some research on your own; learn the history of the wine industry in France, and make a firsthand acquaintance with the wines themselves.

GERMAN WINES

To grow grapes in Germany is an uphill battle against climate, insects, and vine disease.

German vineyards lie the farthest north of any in the world. The southernmost of them are as far north as Newfoundland. Because of the chill, grapes can only be grown on sunny hillsides along river valleys, and only a few of the hardiest varieties can be grown at all.

Those that win over these odds do triumph, in more than their fight for life. Some wine lovers consider the top German white wines to be the best in the world. They seem to have a special character of their own, light and refreshing, often with a fragrant fruitiness. Some of Germany's highest ranked white wines are also quite sweet, such as *Trockenbeerenauslese*.

The Rhine is the fountainhead of German wines. Its valleys and the valleys of its tributaries are the major wine-producing districts.

The vineyards of the Rhine itself break into three regions. From north to south, they are the Rheingau, Rheinhessen, and Rheinpfalz. Wines from the Rheingau possess the qualities most prized, the highest fruit acidity, and most of the hard-to-capture characteristics of style and nobility.

The Rheinhessen produces wines that are less acid than the Rheingaus. Liebfraumilch often comes from the Rheinhessen, although this is a general name that can be applied to Rhine wines lacking a specific appellation.

The Rheinpfalz or Palatinate is the largest producer of these three districts, producing the lightest of the Rhine wines. It also produces some of Germany's best, having a fullness, flavor, and bouquet the Germans call "the Pfalz wine character."

The Moselle is the Rhine's most important tributary, producing wine of equal but different character. The Moselle has two tributaries of its own, the Saar and Ruwer, and Moselle-Saar-Ruwer are often considered as one area, and shown as such on the label. The lightest German wines of all come from the Moselle. Its distinctive quality is credited to the slate soil of the area. Moselblümchen is a general name for Moselle wine that lacks a specific appellation.

Two other tributaries of the Rhine play an important part in German wine production. They are the Nahe and the Main. Both produce distinctive wines.

The Main winds through Franconia, a region that gives us the only German wine bottle that varies from the tall, slender Rhine and Moselle prototype. *Frankenweine* come in a stumpy flagon shape instead.

German Wine Labels: There is so much information on a German label that, unless you know the language or have a guidebook in one hand, you may even feel that it tells you more than you want to know!

Here is a rundown of German label language:

1. Vintage year. The vintage will be printed either on the neck band or label.

2. Classification. A labeling law, passed in 1971, requires that class be shown. You will find *Deutscher Tafelwein* (German table wine, ordinary wine of which little is exported), *Qualitätswein* (quality wine which must originate from certain geographic areas and have reached a minimum alcoholic strength through natural sugar) and *Qualitätswein mit Prädikat* (quality wines with special attributes). These attributes will also be spelled out on the label, such as the following grades, listed in ascending order:

—*Kabinett*—Wine made only from fully matured grapes, without added sugar, from a very limited district. This wine must pass more stringent standards than those in the *Qualitätswein* class.

—*Spätlese* (late harvest)—Wine made from grapes picked after completion of the normal harvest. These grapes have an even higher degree of maturity, giving the wine fuller flavor and fruitiness.

—*Auslese* (selective harvest)—Wine made from only the best bunches of grapes, which are pressed separately from the rest.

—*Beerenauslese (berry selection)*—Wine made from grapes in this classification and the next have the highest degree of concentration of sugar and flavor.

—*Trockenbeerenauslese* (dry berry selection)—Grapes used for this wine have ripened to the point where they are shrunk to a raisin-like dryness. Some say these grapes make the finest wine in the world.

3. Village and vineyard names. On better quality wines, the village name, with the suffix -*er,* is given,

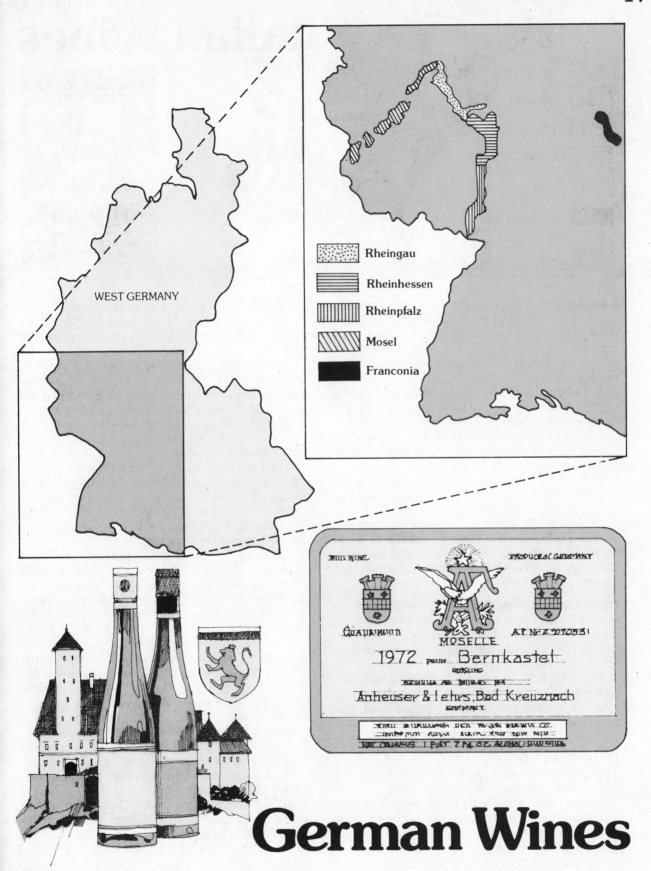

WEST GERMANY

Rheingau
Rheinhessen
Rheinpfalz
Mosel
Franconia

STILL WINE   PRODUCE OF GERMANY

MOSELLE
QUALITÄTSWEIN   A.P. Nr 2 9090531
1972   Bernkastel
RIESLING

Anheuser & Fehrs, Bad Kreuznach
GERMANY

German Wines

Canard à l'Orange (Roast Duckling with Orange Sauce);
Petits Pois (New Peas) in Rice Ring

Italian Wines

Piedmont

Tuscany

Umbria

Marches

Campania

Sicily

followed by the name of the vineyard. Supposing you find the words *Oestricher Doosberg* prominent on a label. That would mean that the wine came from the Doosberg vineyard at Oestrich. The exception to this rule is the vineyard so famous that it needs no village name or identity.

4. Estate bottled. The notation *Eigene Abfüllung* means "bottled by the producer" and *aus eigenem Lesegut* means "from the producer's own estate."

5. Official approval number. *Prüf-Nr.* followed by letters and numbers are the wine's test number, found on quality wines.

6. Growing area. Germany's most famous growing areas, those discussed above, may be shown on the label.

7. Variety. The name of the grape is sometimes, but not always, shown. Riesling is usually the grape grown in the Rheingau and Moselle areas, but many others are grown in Germany, such as the Sylvaner, Traminer, and Müller-Thurgau.

Other German Wine Names: Liebfraumilch is a name that can be applied to any Rhine wine without a specific appellation. Moselblümchen is a similar catch-all title for wines from the Moselle that have no special appellation.

The original May wine is a light Rhine wine into which leaves of the herb woodruff have been infused. It is often served from a punch bowl, garnished with strawberries or other fruit.

ITALIAN WINES

The vine is entwined in Italy's history, and wine production has been part of her life for centuries.

One approach to studying Italian wines is to learn where they come from. Let's take a quick tour of some of the vineyards.

A few small villages tucked into the mountains of

the Piedmont just south of Switzerland produce most of Italy's finest wines. The red Barolo, Barbaresco, and the sparkling Asti Spumante are among the most respected.

Moving on to Tuscany, pay a visit to the homeland of Chianti, that robust red so familiar in its straw-colored flask. That flask, by the way, is your clue that this wine is not meant for aging. The round-bottomed bottle just won't store in a bin. Such chianti should be enjoyed young—it goes downhill after a couple of years.

A distinguished relative, Chianti Classico, is something else. Estate-bottled Chianti Classico comes in a straight-sided bottle and does improve with age. Look for the seal with the black rooster on a golden background. It's the sign of this special wine, produced between Florence and Siena.

Traveling down south of Florence, you'll find Soave and Orvieto, white wines of the Umbrian Hills. There are red wines in this region, too. These are Bardolino and Valpolicella, two reds with a difference. They are so light that they are recommended to accompany white meats as well as red.

From the Marches of the Adriatic coast comes the dry white Verdicchio dei Castelli di Jesi. Another wine with a name significant for Christians is the famous Lacrima Christi (tears of Christ). This wine originated on the slopes of Mt. Vesuvius in the Campania region and is really not just one wine but several. It comes in dry, sweet, and sparkling types.

Italy's famous dessert wine, Marsala, is produced off the mainland on the island of Sicily.

Confronted with a bottle of Italian wine, you may expect to find this information:

1. The name of the wine. Generic names are based on geographic area, such as Chianti or Valpolicella. Varietal names are based on the variety of grape, such as Barbera or Verdicchio. A varietal

Spanish Wines

SPAIN

Jerez

Rioja

La Mancha

FINO
SACRIOSI
EXTRA DRY
COCKTAIL
SHERRY

JEREZ, SPAIN
IMPORTED

name is sometimes combined with a geographic designation such as Barbera (the grape) d'Alba (from Alba).

2. The name of the producer (*Produceri*). The producer's name may be shown in connection with the town. Frequently it is shown in connection with his cellars (*cantina*), the wine house (*casa vinicola*), estate (*tenementi* or *tenuta*) or cooperative producer (*cantina sociale*).

3. DOC (*Denominazione di Origine Controllata*). This notation guarantees that the wine is made of specific grapes from a designated area, according to government decree in 1963. It is administered by a "jury of wine peers," the Italian National Committee for the Protection of the Denomination of Origin of Wines.

4. Vintage year. If the vintage is shown, it will be on the main or shoulder label.

5. The grower's consortia seal. This seal appears as a further guarantee of control. If a bottle number is shown, it indicates that the production is limited.

6. Bottler. Bottling usually takes place at or near the production area. Such words as *Imbottigliato* (bottled), *Infiascato* (put in flasks), *In zona d'origine* (at the growing area), and *Nello stabilimento* (at the producer's premises) all refer to bottling.

7. *Classico*. This word, used after the wine name, such as Chianti Classico, means that the wine comes from the original heartland of a production area. There are twenty provincial regions, each producing a *classico* version of its wine.

SPANISH WINES

If you are looking for a fine, authentic Spanish wine you are probably looking for a sherry. The original version comes from Jerez; the British changed the name to conform to their pronunciation.

But Spain produces many other wines besides sherry. The number of acres devoted to vineyards in Spain is among the highest in the world, but the harsh, dry climate has resulted in a lower production yield than that of France or Italy.

Sherry country is located between the cities of Cadiz and Seville on the southern coast of Spain in the region of Andalusia. Under the *Denominacion de Origen* (place-name) regulations, the sherry vineyards lie around the town of Jerez-de-la-Frontera.

There are many other place names for Spanish wines, since so much of the country is planted in vineyards. Some of the best table wines come from Rioja in the north. Rioja is named for the Rio Oja, a small tributary of the River Ebro. This is in chilly upland country, well suited to growing grapes somewhat like those of the Bordeaux country in France.

The wines of Rioja are often compared to those of Bordeaux, and it is no accident that there are similarities. When the phylloxera plague hit the Bordeaux vineyards in the 1880s, many French wine families moved to the then-unaffected Ebro Valley and settled in what is now the center of the Rioja wine area. They took with them their Bordeaux know-how and applied it to the conditions they found in Spain. The finest of the resulting wine, particularly the red, has won fans around the world.

The wine regions in central Spain south of Madrid include part of La Mancha, the territory made memorable by Don Quixote. La Mancha is also one of the place-names of the area, as is Manzanares. The extensive vineyards of central Spain produce mainly *vino corriente* (inexpensive, everyday table wine).

Catalonia, in the northeast, has its share of place-names, too. Among them are Malvasia de Sitges, Tarragona, and Barcelona.

Dropping down the east coast, we arrive at vine-

Greek Wines

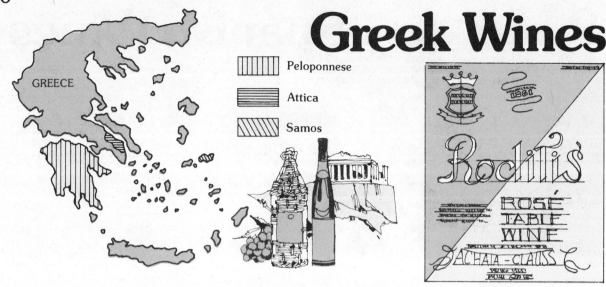

GREECE

- ▥ Peloponnese
- ▤ Attica
- ▨ Samos

yards with the place-name of Alicante. Red table wines are the main product here.

Over in the northwest, the Rueda country is a big producer of dry white wines. Nearby Toro is better known for reds.

Despite Spain's prodigious output of table wines, one is drawn back to the subject of dessert and appetizer wines when seeking the source of her greatness. Sherry heads the list, followed by Montilla, Manzanilla (both relatives of sherry), and Malaga. Sherry itself should be considered as a family rather than a single wine, and its variations range from dry to sweet.

The Spanish Sherry Label: The notation *fino* on sherry means a wine that is quite free from sweetness, and pale to slightly amber in color. Sherry labeled *fino amontillado* is deeper colored and not quite so dry. *Oloroso* is deeper yet in color and often sweetened to suit buyer tastes. *Oloroso* is definitely a dessert wine; the dry sherries are appetizer wines. All sherries are fortified with brandy to bring the alcoholic content up to around 17 percent.

Other Label Language: The *Denominacion de Origen*—Somewhat like the *Appellation Contrôllée* in France, this term designates the growing area and usually implies a quality wine.

Consejo Regulador—An organization for the control, defense, and promotion of a *Denominacion de Origen*.

Reserva—Mature quality wine.

GREEK WINES

The gods that dwelt on Mount Olympus had a healthy respect for wine. They even had a special emissary, Dionysus, to spread the good news about wine to the world! In a subtle way, Dionysus is still at work. Tending vineyards and making wine (to say

nothing of drinking it) are still part of Grecian life.

Although Greece produces red, rosé, and white wines, the one most distinctively Greek is retsina, a white wine to which sandarac has been added. If your impression is that it tastes a little like varnish, your taste buds are right on target—sandarac is a pine resin used also to make varnish! Yet Greeks have cherished this unusual wine for thousands of years, and it has picked up fans elsewhere. If you plan a Greek wine tasting, do include a retsina for its conversational value.

The chalky soil of the Greek mainland and several of the islands is well suited to vineyards, and the dry climate favors a sweet grape. Wine in Greece is plentiful, and often inexpensive, but is generally not in the running for the luxury trade.

The Peloponnese, the southern peninsula of Greece, is one of Greece's busiest wine-producing areas. The best known wines of the Peloponnese are the sweet wines; Mavrodaphne, a sweet, dark wine, is considered one of the best.

Retsina comes mainly from Attica, the region in which Athens is located. The scenic Greek isles also produce their share of wine. The island Samos produces a sweet Muscat that is well known. Samos has one of the few place-names protected by Greek law.

Greek wine labels are not difficult to read, as the ones for export to this country are printed in English. The volume and the alcoholic content are shown, as are the producers and importers.

There may be a notation such as "red (or pink, or white) table wine," and sometimes notes on a back label regarding proper serving temperature. Here are a few guidelines to the Greek words you may find:
—*Roditis*—Rosé table wine
—*Demestica*—White or red table wine; also *oinos lefkos* (white wine) and *oinos erythros* (red wine)
—*Afrothes*—Sparkling wine

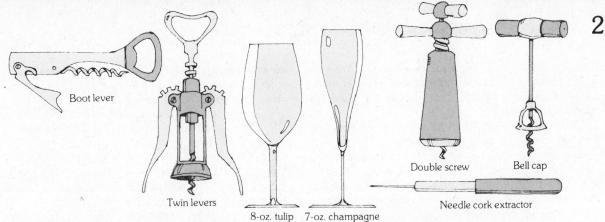

Boot lever

Twin levers

8-oz. tulip   7-oz. champagne

Double screw   Bell cap

Needle cork extractor

WINE ACCESSORIES AND WINE MANNERS

So you've brought home the wine—now, what to do with it! First order of business is storing it.

THE WINE CELLAR

If you're lucky enough to have a spare closet or a corner in the basement, you can build your own wine-storage shelf. Wine that does not require aging can be stored standing up. Store bottles lying down if wine is to be aged. A notched board set at right angles to the storage shelf will permit bottles to lie on their sides without bumping each other.

IDEAL CONDITIONS FOR THE WINE CELLAR

Temperature in a wine cellar should be between 55° to 60°F; 45° to 70°F are outer limits. Humidity should be high, because dry air dries out corks and leads to wine spoilage. A dark location is best. Vibration is bad, especially for aged wines which have thrown a sediment. Don't locate your wine storage too near laundry or other equipment that vibrates.

THE WINE RECORD

People who lay down wine for future use are advised to keep a wine record. Make a note of where and when you bought the wine; later record when and to whom it was served, with your comments.

CORKSCREWS

It's not necessary to pay a lot to get a good, practical bottle opener. You can do the job with an inexpensive one.

The metal spiral that is twisted into the cork is called the "worm"; it should be about 2½ inches long. The point should be off center, but aligned with the spiral.

One of the simplest of corkscrews is the waiter's *boot lever*. The worm is twisted into the cork, and the end of the jack lever is fixed into position on the lip of the bottle. To raise the cork, lift the end of the handle. The advantage of this corkscrew is that it folds flat and can be carried in a pocket.

Another common corkscrew is the *bell cap*. Twist the worm into the cork, and the cork raises up into the bell as you continue to turn the handle. To remove the cork from the bottle, first rock the handle, then give it a pull to release the cork.

A style that gives good leverage is the *twin lever* opener. Once the worm is in, simply push down on the two "arms" to draw up the cork.

With the *double screw* opener, the worm is inserted by turning the small upper handle. Then the lower handle turns on wooden threads in the same direction to remove the cork.

The *needle cork extractor* is a newer style. A needle goes through the cork, and through it air is pumped. If all goes well, the cork will be forced out. If the cork does not rise after pumping, it may be stuck, and you should go back to the old familiar corkscrew to finish the job. Pumps have been known to explode weak bottles.

GLASSES

Once upon a time each wine had its own special glass. But mobility and limited storage space have made that custom, like the full-fledged wine cellar, a thing of the past.

Wine does show off at its best in the proper glass but one style of wine glass for all is sufficient.

The glass most generally approved is the stemmed 8- or 9-ounce tulip-shaped glass. This glass, filled half full or less, offers plenty of room for the wine to "breathe" and for you to breathe in its bouquet.

The stem allows you to hold the glass without

warming the wine. In those cases when you wish to warm the wine to release more of the bouquet, such as when drinking brandy, the bowl of the glass fits nicely into your hand.

Clear glass is better than tinted, as it lets you see the true color and clarity of the wine.

The tall, tulip glass is suitable for champagne, too, although some people prefer a slimmer 7-ounce glass. Its smaller surface area lets the champagne bubble up more attractively than the saucer shape often used for champagne.

WAYS WITH WINE

Traditions have grown up around the use of wine and make up our wine heritage.

While not a "ten commandments," each of the following wine rules was established for some reason and together they made wine usage more enjoyable for the founders. Wine traditions can be broken to achieve some special effect, but you can get away with this more successfully if you are first familiar with them.

1. Serve dry wines before sweet. Sweet flavors dull the taste buds and lessen the appreciation of whatever follows.

2. Serve light-bodied wines before full-bodied ones. ("Body" describes thickness or thinness of the liquid.)

3. Serve white wines before red wines. This applies only to a formal meal where a selection of wines is appropriate, or to wine tastings. For everyday meals only one wine is needed—the one that goes best with the meat.

4. Champagne may be served at any point before, during, or after a meal.

5. White wines usually accompany fish and white meats such as veal, poultry, and sometimes pork.

6. Red wines usually accompany red meats such as beef, lamb, pork, and game birds and meats.

7. At a meal, serve a wine that is similar to the one used in the food preparation. It need not be exactly the same. Few people would cook with an expensive, vintage Bordeaux or Burgundy wine. But in preparing the accompanying dish, a generic claret or burgundy—one that is pleasing enough to drink—should be used.

8. Some wines are best served chilled, others at room temperature. Appetizer wines and white and rosé table wines should be chilled an hour in the refrigerator or 15 minutes in an ice bath. Icy temperatures interfere with full flavor.

Red wines and dessert wines are served at "room temperature," but when the custom originated, rooms were rarely as warm as we keep them today, except in summer, of course! Sixty degrees F is recommended; 70 degrees F is usually considered tops for wine temperature. That's the advantage of a cool cellar for storage. On a hot August day, better chill all wine, at least to 70 degrees F.

Sparkling wines are always served chilled.

9. Uncork red wine about an hour before serving so it can "breathe."

10. Omit wine with the salad course when the dressing is vinegary, and when serving spicy dishes such as curry. The sourness of the vinegar, as well as the spice, does battle with the wine flavor.

Other traditions of serving wine, like the above guidelines, have grown up over the years. Take the routine of the wine waiter in the restaurant. He will offer the cork to the host to sniff. This may not only seem silly to the uninitiated; it may not be completely understood by the host who has been through it many times.

The cork is offered because, on rare occasions, it will be bad. And if the end of a bad cork has touched the wine, it has probably given the wine a bad flavor. "Corkiness" is the term used for the cork disease that leads to that flavor. More common than corkiness is wine spoilage resulting from a dry, shrivelled cork that has allowed too much air to reach the wine. In either case, the wine should be rejected.

Do not send back a bottle because of mold at the top end of the cork. Mold isn't attractive, but it's the natural result of storage in a damp cellar. A dry cellar would cause worse problems if it allowed the cork to dry and admit air. To prevent air from entering, corked wine is laid on its side so the liquid keeps the cork wet and air out. Wine capped with metal or plastic can be stored standing up.

But back to our wine waiter. After presenting the cork, he pours a little wine in the host's glass and shows him the label. This, plus the taste test, assures the host that the wine really is the one he ordered, and that the taste is up to expectations. There rarely is cause for rejection.

At home, the host can observe tradition by pouring a little wine into his own glass first, and sampling. More than a formality, this will put any cork fragments into his glass, not a guest's.

The host serves the wine moving clockwise around the table, serving the women first, then returning to serve the men. Wine glasses are not lifted from the table as the wine is poured: a little twist after pouring should catch the remaining drop as the bottle is lifted. For extra security, you can buy a special wine-pouring bottle top that insures the wine will go where you want it. A towel around the bottle is a little too showy, and besides, it hides the label.

As for guest manners, smoking inhibits the full appreciation of wine bouquet and flavor, not only for the smoker but for those around him. Save the cigarettes and cigars for after dinner.

AN ENTERTAINING IDEA
A WINE TASTING

"A loaf of bread, a jug of wine, and thou . . ." are all it takes for a twosome. And it's not such a bad formula for a party, as anyone who has been to a wine tasting knows.

When the object of a gathering is to learn about wine, food should be secondary. A loaf of bread would, indeed, fill the bill. Or cheese and crackers. But in practice, the hostess usually likes to prepare something, either for accompaniment or follow-up to the tasting.

The selection of wines should rate the highest priority in planning. Giving a theme to the tasting adds to the interest. Here are a few ideas:

AMERICAN WINES WITH THEIR EUROPEAN COUNTERPARTS

Serve American wines named for famous European wines. Serve the European prototype with them to see how close the relationship, if any.

The tasting might feature all white wines, all reds, or a combination. If you choose a combination, serve the white wines before the red. The red wines will benefit from a breathing spell while you taste the whites.

For this party, you might select two or more American wines called "Rhine," from various states, along with a German Rhine wine. Follow up with American wines labeled "Burgundy" and the real thing from France.

SHERRY TASTING

Serve dry American sherries from California and eastern states for comparison with Spanish sherry.

Among the Spanish, Tio Pepe and La Ina are excellent choices. Conclude with sweet sherries.

SPARKLING WINE TASTING

All that sparkles is not champagne. In France, the only wine that can bear the title is grown in a legally delimited area. Other sparkling wines of France are called *vins mousseux*, with a variety of specific trade names. Sample them alongside the sparkling Sekt of Germany, the Asti Spumante of Italy, and other foreign sparkling wines. Be sure to include one or more of the fine American champagnes. The *pièce de résistance* of the tasting should be an example of the French original.

SPOTLIGHT WINES OF ONE COUNTRY

Another idea is to serve a selection of representative wines from one country. The country you choose will determine the wines you feature. For example, if it's Germany, you'll emphasize or limit the choice to white wines. If it's Spain, you may wish to concentrate on sherries. Focusing on one nation provides a theme that can be carried out in invitations, decorations, and even a musical background.

PREPARATIONS FOR THE TASTING

Once you've decided how many to invite, you can work out details for giving the party. If the guest list is large and you have plenty of room, you might set up three or four serving stations for the wine.

Eight wines are the upper limit to serve at a wine tasting. And servings should be small; no more than an ounce the first time around, so that taste buds are not overwhelmed by so much alcohol that they are unable to distinguish differences.

The host and hostess should pour for each guest, or if it is more convenient, pour several servings in advance. If you've done a little research on the wine, this is a good time to share it with your guests.

If the guest list is small, the host may introduce the wines one at a time and serve in the living room. However you decide to serve the wine, leave the bottle out so guests can examine the label.

The exception to this format is the "blind tasting" when the purpose is to see which wine a group prefers. Score cards are often provided for "votes." Bottles are tied into sacks with just the neck exposed, or the label is covered in some other way.

Blind tastings can be fun, if it's understood that there is no "right" or "wrong" choice. By keeping an open mind, one may find that a wine with less status (and price) delivers all the enjoyment of a more prestigious label.

Obviously, glassware is important at a wine tasting. It's not always necessary to have a separate glass for each wine; a container to catch the remnants of one sample before starting another makes it possible to use just one glass for a complete tasting. But having more than one glass per guest permits him to compare two or more wines side by side.

Liquor stores sometimes rent glassware or provide it free of charge with a sale. Plastic glassware is another economical solution.

It is important that the glassware be uncolored and without ornamentation so that the wine can be examined easily. Stemmed glassware permits the taster to hold the wine without warming it.

THE TASTING

The sense of taste is a prime consideration at a wine tasting, but when judging a wine's character, the other senses are to be consulted, too. The sense of sight and smell play critical roles.

The professional wine tasters give great weight to the appearance of the wine. They examine it in the glass, holding it up to the light. They check the color and clarity; cloudiness is considered a drawback. They spin the wine around in the glass and watch as it trickles down. The trail it leaves is called "legs" or "cathedral windows." This is a key to the viscosity or body of the wine.

Warming the wine in the palm of the hand releases the bouquet of the wine; the bouquet is the wine's "nose" and the taster inhales it before he sips.

When actually tasting the wine, the pro goes through a gurgling ritual that gives him certain taste sensations in various parts of the mouth. Few of us are secure, or extroverted enough, to carry this off in public. But do sip slowly and give all the taste impressions a chance to register. Whether or not you put out score cards is a matter of preference; don't make it a burden.

WHAT TO SERVE AT A TASTING

To let the wine star as it should at a tasting, food should be incidental. Cheese and crackers are the classic wine-tasting accompaniments; a bit of each after one wine sample helps to prepare the palate for the next. Pair mild cheese with delicate wines (such as Swiss and Gruyère with light, white wines) and sharper cheeses with full-bodied wines (such as Cheddar and Edam with red wines).

But many hostesses take pride in serving something they've prepared, too. The following recipes are all appropriate. Staying in the simple cheese-bread category, the cheese bread, gougere, is nice with wine, and so is the quiche. Both are French in origin. The tyropitas are Greek, but all three complement the wines of any country.

Such a menu is adequate, but if you wish, conclude with coffee and dessert. The best party dessert is one that can be made well in advance, then stored until serving time so that full attention can be given to the wine tasting itself. Cheesecake, your guests may be interested to know, has a Greek heritage, but the version given here is as American as apple pie.

Gougere

1 cup milk
¼ cup butter or margarine
1 teaspoon salt
4 to 5 drops Tabasco
1 cup all-purpose flour
4 eggs
1 cup (4 ounces) cubed Swiss or
    Gruyère cheese
    Milk for brushing

1. Combine milk, butter, salt, and Tabasco in a heavy saucepan. Bring to a boil. Remove from heat.
2. Add flour, all at once, to mixture in saucepan. Stir until it forms a ball. Return to heat and stir vigorously about 25 strokes until the dough clears the sides of the pan and spoon. Remove from heat.
3. Transfer dough to large mixer bowl. Beat on low speed; add an egg and continue beating until dough looks shiny and egg is completely incorporated. Repeat with remaining eggs, one at a time.

4. Fold in cheese, reserving a few pieces for top.

5. Into well-greased 9-inch pie pan, drop dough by tablespoonfuls into large egg shapes around the sides to form a ring. Brush with milk and sprinkle on reserved cubes of cheese for topping.

6. Bake at 450°F for 20 minutes, without opening the oven. Reduce heat to 350°F and bake 20 minutes longer. Reduce heat to 325°F and bake 10 minutes longer. May be served hot or cold.

One 9-inch round loaf

Cheese Appetizer Pies, Greek Style (Tyropitas)

1 pound butter
1 pound feta cheese
1 pound baker's cheese
4 or 5 eggs
1 pound filo (phyllo) pastry
    or strudel leaves—available
    at specialty shops

1. Melt butter. Keep over low heat while mixing other ingredients.

2. Chop feta cheese into large mixing bowl. Stir in baker's cheese gently so that cheeses are mixed but still retain identity. Add 4 or 5 eggs, depending upon size, so that cheese mixture is moist but not runny.

3. Unfold filo dough. Cut in half lengthwise, then in half again to make 4 long strips. Place dough on waxed paper; cover with a second sheet of waxed paper and a slightly damp tea towel so that dough does not dry out. (If towel is too wet, leaves may stick together.)

4. For each cheese pie, remove one strip of dough to a separate sheet of waxed paper. Using a large pastry brush or new paint brush, brush one side of dough with melted butter.

5. Place a teaspoonful of cheese mixture at the center of the top narrow edge of dough. Dividing dough in imaginary thirds lengthwise, fold right third over center third, then fold left third over right and center thirds. Brush entire folded strip with butter.

6. Starting at the top of the strip containing the cheese mixture, fold dough into a triangular shape as if folding a flag. Alternate folding right corner to left edge, then left corner to right edge. The initial triangle is a little tricky to form, but once folded, the later triangles smooth out in shape.

7. Make each folding edge by pushing lightly with brush against the formed triangle, then fold triangle over remaining flat dough. Don't fold too tightly or pies won't puff when baked.

8. If dough should tear while folding the strip, use a little melted butter on the brush to "glue" it together.

9. When you reach the end of the strip, put a little extra butter on the remaining dough and fold it over the triangle. The butter should hold it in place.

10. Freeze cheese pies in freezer containers, putting waxed paper or foil between layers. Wrap well.

11. At serving time, place unthawed cheese pies on ungreased baking sheets with sides or in cake pans (butter will leak slightly).

12. Bake at 350°F for 10 to 15 minutes, or until golden. Serve hot.

About 80 to 100 appetizer pies

Swiss Cheese-Onion Quiche

6 slices bacon
1 cup chopped onion
1 unbaked 9-inch pie shell
½ pound Swiss cheese, cut into
  ½-inch cubes
3 eggs, slightly beaten
½ cup milk
¼ cup dairy sour cream
½ teaspoon salt
  Dash pepper

1. Fry bacon until crisp and drain on paper towels.
2. Pour off all but 1 tablespoon bacon drippings from skillet. Stir-fry chopped onion in drippings until tender; drain.
3. Crumble bacon into bottom of pie shell. Add onion and cheese cubes evenly over the bacon.
4. Combine beaten eggs, milk, sour cream, salt, and pepper in mixing bowl. Pour over bacon-onion-cheese mixture in pie shell.
5. Bake at 375°F for 25 to 30 minutes, or until center is set. Do not overbake.

One 9-inch pie

Cheesecake

9 slices zwieback, coarsely
  crushed (about 1 cup crumbs)
⅔ cup sugar
4 tablespoons butter or margarine
1 pound cream cheese
1 teaspoon grated lemon peel
1 tablespoon lemon juice
5 eggs, separated

1. Place zwieback between layers of waxed paper or aluminum foil and crush with rolling pin; mix with 2 teaspoons of the sugar and the butter. Work with your hands until ingredients are blended well. Put zwieback into a 9-inch springform pan and press firmly on bottom, using back of tablespoon.
2. Soften the cream cheese and beat in remaining sugar, a small amount at a time; beat in lemon peel, lemon juice, and egg yolks. Continue beating until fluffy.
3. Beat egg whites until stiff peaks are formed. Gently fold into cream cheese mixture until thoroughly blended. Turn mixture into pan over zwieback crust.
4. Bake at 300°F about 75 minutes, or until filling is "set." Remove from oven and cool on a rack about 10 minutes before removing rim from springform pan. Allow cheesecake to rest about 3 hours before serving.

8 to 10 servings

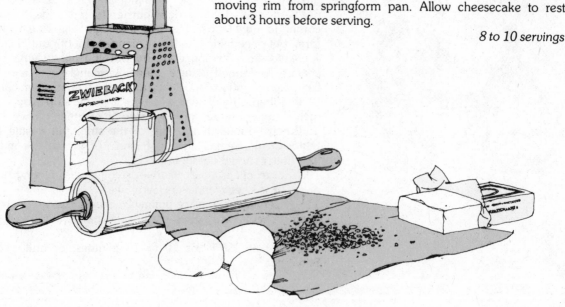

AN ENTERTAINING IDEA
A WINE-AND-DINE CLUB

By a sort of alchemy anyone can practice, wine can add glitter to an ordinary meal. But when the meal is special, wine belongs as much as china and silver.

There is a real art to producing a special-occasion meal. Expertise comes with experience, and some people have formed clubs to learn together.

ORGANIZING A GROUP

The size of a dinner group is usually limited by the number you can seat and serve comfortably—generally no more than eight or ten. This number, or four or five couples, can also divide the menu chores conveniently, each bringing one course, with the hostess responsible for the main course.

BLUEPRINT FOR A GOURMET DINNER

The theme and elements of the menu should be coordinated. Don't trust to pot-luck if you want to achieve an effect. Having a theme, such as foods from one country, is far better.

THE APPETIZER COURSE

Whatever the theme, an appetizer course belongs in your plan. Served in the living room, it provides something for the early arrivals, and gets the conversational wheels turning.

Appetizers, to live up to their name, should merely whet the appetite. Vegetables, cooked and marinated as in the Italian antipasto tray, or served fresh in strips with a dip, are ample.

The wine with the appetizer should be light. According to the old rule, very often a white wine is served as the aperitif, followed by a fuller-bodied red wine at the table.

THE SOUP COURSE

Once the party has gathered and appetites are thoroughly ready for the feast, the scene shifts to the dining room. If the hostess has fancy serving plates, these are resplendent at each place. And if she also has a pretty tureen, it will be placed before the host.

Depending upon the choice of soup, a wine may or may not be served with it. Sometimes the wine is served *in* the soup.

THE FISH COURSE

In an elegant menu, fish follows the soup. Because it comes just before the main entree, it should be harmonious with it. A dry white wine is customary with the fish course.

THE ENTREE

The main course is the hub of the menu around which the other courses fit. The choice of theme for the evening will determine the entree. Roast duck with orange sauce, for example, would suit a French theme, just as souvlakia fits a Greek dinner. Try to find recipes that are as true to the source as possible—they will make your gourmet dinners authentic.

The wine to accompany the entree will depend upon the choice of meat. Often the most full-bodied and finest quality wine of the evening will be served at this time.

THE SALAD COURSE

In some cuisines, the salad accompanies the meat course. In others, there may be a separate course, as for example, the salad served after the entree in a French menu.

The greens for your salad should be very crisp and cold. Wash and tear them before the guests arrive. The trick of wrapping them in a tea towel and refrigerating will keep them cold and dry. Don't add dressing until serving time for a crisp, succulent salad.

Because vinegary dressings are heavy competition, wine is usually omitted from the salad course.

THE CHEESE COURSE
This course offers breathing space between the heavier entree and a more elaborate dessert. Wine is expected with this course as it is so harmonious with cheese. A sweeter wine, perhaps the same as that to be served with dessert, goes well with many cheeses.

THE DESSERT COURSE
You may plan as elegant a dessert as you wish. Just remember when planning that you will have worked your way through several substantial courses, and the edge will have been well worn from most appetites.

Something light, a fancy mousse, perhaps, or a fruit compote may be the perfect cap for your dining experience. A sweet wine will be a fitting partner—consider a cream sherry, tawny port, or a sparkling wine.

FRENCH DINNER MENU

Course	Wine
APPETIZER	
Pâté de Foie de Volaille (Poultry Liver Paste) with Melba Toast	**Champagne**
Canapés de Crevettes (Shrimp Canapés)	
SOUP	
Soupe à l'Oignon (Onion Soup)	**Beaujolais**
ENTREE	
Canard à l'Orange (Roast Duckling with Orange Sauce)	**Pomerol**
Petits Pois (New Peas) in Rice Ring	
SALAD	
Salade à la Crème (Green Salad with Cream Dressing)	
CHEESE	
Tray of Camembert, Brie, Port Salut, and Roquefort	**Haut-Médoc**
DESSERT	
Pêches Melba (Peaches with Vanilla Ice Cream and Raspberry Purée)	**Sauternes**
Coffee	**Cognac**

Pâté de Foie de Volaille (Poultry Liver Paste)

2 tablespoons salt pork fat
1 cup uncooked duck or chicken
   livers
1 teaspoon salt
¼ teaspoon thyme
¼ teaspoon freshly ground pepper
1 bay leaf
¼ cup sherry

1. Heat fat until very hot, then add remaining ingredients except sherry. Cook 3 to 4 minutes. Remove bay leaf.
2. Rub livers through a sieve. Blend sieved liver well with sherry.

About 1 cup paste

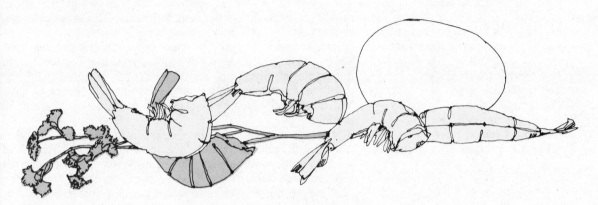

Canapés de Crevettes (Shrimp Canapés)

18 canned, or cooked and peeled,
   shrimp
2 tablespoons butter
1 egg
12 crisp crackers
¼ cup mayonnaise or French
   dressing
1 tablespoon finely chopped parsley

1. Chill 12 shrimp in refrigerator. Finely chop remaining 6; add and blend in butter well.
2. Hard-cook egg. Force egg yolk through sieve and set aside. Reserve egg white for other use.
3. Spread shrimp butter onto crackers.
4. Dip the whole shrimp into mayonnaise or French dressing.
5. Place on shrimp-buttered crackers. Sprinkle over shrimp about ¼ teaspoon each of sieved egg yolk and chopped parsley.

12 canapés

Soupe à l'Oignon (Onion Soup)

3 large onions, thinly sliced
½ cup butter or vegetable oil
1½ tablespoons flour
5½ cups seasoned meat stock
   Few drops Tabasco
   Salt and pepper to taste
6 slices toast
4 ounces grated Cheddar cheese

1. Fry onions gently in oil until golden brown. Stir in flour, then stock and seasonings; simmer 10 minutes.
2. Pour soup into individual ovenproof dishes, put a slice of toast on top, and cover with cheese. Broil 3 to 4 minutes until cheese is melted and bubbly.

6 servings

Canard à l'Orange
(Roast Duckling with Orange Sauce)

2 ducklings (4 to 5 pounds each)
2 teaspoons salt
½ teaspoon pepper
1 clove garlic, peeled and cut
  crosswise into halves
½ cup dry white wine
½ cup orange marmalade
Sauce:
2 tablespoons butter or margarine
1 can (13¾ ounces) condensed
  chicken broth
½ cup orange marmalade
¼ cup dry white wine
¼ cup orange juice
2 teaspoons cornstarch
2 teaspoons lemon juice
2 tablespoons slivered orange peel

1. If frozen, let ducklings thaw according to package directions. Remove giblets, necks, and livers from ducklings. Reserve livers for sauce; if desired, reserve giblets and necks for soup stock. Remove and discard excess fat. Wash, drain, and pat dry with paper toweling. Rub cavities with salt, pepper, and garlic. Fasten neck skin of each to back with a skewer. Tuck tail ends into cavities. Tie legs together and tuck wing tips under ducklings. Prick skin generously to release fat. Place ducklings, breast side up, on a rack in a large shallow roasting pan.
2. Roast at 350°F 2 to 2½ hours or until legs can be moved easily, basting several times during roasting and removing accumulated drippings about every 30 minutes. Remove ducklings from oven and spread surface with mixture of wine and marmalade. Return to oven and continue roasting for 10 minutes.
3. For sauce, melt butter in a skillet. Add duckling livers and sauté until lightly browned. Remove and chop livers. Add chicken broth, marmalade, wine, orange juice, and cornstarch blended with lemon juice. Cook, stirring constantly over low heat for 10 minutes or until sauce bubbles and thickens. Stir in chopped livers and orange peel.
4. Transfer ducklings to a heated platter. Remove skewers and twine. Garnish, if desired, with watercress and orange slices. Reheat sauce if necessary and serve with duckling.

8 servings

Petits Pois (New Peas) in Rice Ring

1 package (6 or 6¾ ounces)
  seasoned wild and white rice mix
3 pounds fresh peas
  Butter

1. Cook rice mix according to package directions.
2. Meanwhile, rinse and shell peas just before cooking to retain their delicate flavor. Cook covered in boiling salted water to cover for 15 to 20 minutes or until peas are tender. Drain and add just enough butter so peas glisten.
3. Butter a 1-quart ring mold. When rice is done, turn into the mold, packing down gently with spoon. Invert onto a warm serving platter and lift off mold.
4. Spoon hot peas into center of rice ring just before serving.

About 6 servings

Salade à la Crème (Green Salad with Cream Dressing)

1 quart mixed greens (such as
  iceberg, Boston, or Bibb lettuce,
  romaine, escarole, or chicory)
½ cup dairy sour cream
2 tablespoons chopped parsley
2 tablespoons dry white wine
  (such as chenin blanc)
½ teaspoon salt
⅛ teaspoon freshly ground
  pepper

1. Using only perfect leaves, wash, dry, tear into pieces, and chill greens before combining with dressing. Cold, dry leaves ensure a crisp salad.
2. Combine sour cream, parsley, wine, salt, and pepper.
3. At serving time, transfer greens to a large bowl, add dressing, and toss well.

About 6 servings

Pêches Melba
(Peaches with Vanilla Ice Cream and Raspberry Purée)

4 portions vanilla ice cream	1. Place vanilla ice cream in stemmed dessert glasses. Cover with peach halves.
8 canned peach halves, drained	
1½ cups fully ripe raspberries	2. For sauce, rinse raspberries and press through a coarse sieve or food mill. Sweeten with sugar and chill thoroughly.
2 to 4 tablespoons sugar	

4 portions vanilla ice cream
8 canned peach halves, drained
1½ cups fully ripe raspberries
2 to 4 tablespoons sugar
  Whipped cream for garnishing
  Pistachios or toasted slivered
    almonds (optional)

1. Place vanilla ice cream in stemmed dessert glasses. Cover with peach halves.
2. For sauce, rinse raspberries and press through a coarse sieve or food mill. Sweeten with sugar and chill thoroughly.
3. Top peach halves with raspberry sauce. Garnish with whipped cream and nuts, if desired.

4 servings

GERMAN DINNER MENU

Course	*Wine*
APPETIZER	
Rollmops (Rolled Pickled Herring Fillets)	**Gewürztraminer**
Roggenbrot (Buttered Rye Bread)	**(Spicy White Wine)**
SOUP	
Gemüsesuppe (Vegetable Soup)	
ENTREE	
Gefüllter Gänsebraten (Roast Goose with Prune-Apple Stuffing)	**Rheingau Riesling**
	(Rhine Wine)
Nudeln (Buttered Noodles)	
Rotkohl (Sweet-Sour Red Cabbage)	
DESSERT	
Schaumtorte (Meringue Torte)	**Trockenbeerenauslese**
	or Sekt (Sparkling White Wine)
Coffee	

Gemüsesuppe (Vegetable Soup)

1 **soup bone, cracked**
3 **quarts cold water**
1 **tablespoon salt**
1 **pound potatoes (3 medium),
washed, pared, and diced**
1 **pound green beans, washed, ends
cut off and beans cut in halves**
3 **small carrots, washed, pared or
scraped, and cut in quarters
lengthwise**
2 **medium onions, chopped
(about 1 cup)**
2 **stalks celery, cut in ½-inch pieces**
2 **tablespoons minced parsley**
2 **tablespoons sugar**
2 **teaspoons salt**
3 **cans (19 ounces each) tomatoes
(about 6 cups, sieved)**
2 **tablespoons shortening**
¼ **cup flour**
¼ **cup finely chopped onion**

1. Wipe soup bone with a clean, damp cloth. Put into a large saucepot or kettle having a cover along with water and salt.
2. Cover and bring to boiling, reduce heat and simmer 1½ hours. During cooking, occasionally remove foam that forms on top. Meanwhile, prepare vegetables.
3. After 1½ hours, add vegetables to soup with parsley, sugar, and salt. Simmer 30 minutes, or until vegetables are tender.
4. Just before vegetables are tender, force canned tomatoes through a sieve or food mill. Set aside.
5. Heat shortening in a saucepan. Blend in flour.
6. Add chopped onion and cook over low heat, stirring constantly. Cook until mixture bubbles and is lightly browned. Remove from heat and add gradually, stirring constantly, 1 cup of the soup stock.
7. Cook 1 to 2 minutes, or until smooth. Blend into soup with sieved tomatoes. Bring to boiling, reduce heat, and simmer 5 to 10 minutes, or until soup is slightly thickened. Remove soup bone. Serve steaming hot.

8 to 10 servings

Gefüllter Gänsebraten
(Roast Goose with Prune-Apple Stuffing)

2 **cups pitted cooked prunes**
1 **goose (10 to 12 pounds, ready-to-
cook weight)**
   Salt
6 **medium (about 2 pounds)
apples**

1. Set out a shallow roasting pan with rack. Have prunes ready, reserving about 8 to 10 prunes for garnish.
2. If goose is frozen, thaw according to directions on package. Clean and remove any layers of fat from body cavity and opening of goose. Cut off neck at body, leaving on neck skin. Rinse and pat dry with absorbent paper. (Reserve giblets for use in gravy or other food preparation.) Rub body and neck cavities of goose with salt. Wash, core, pare and quarter apples.
3. Lightly fill body and neck cavities with the apples and prunes. To close body cavity, sew or skewer and lace with cord. Fasten neck skin to back with skewer. Loop cord around legs and tighten slightly. Place breast side down on rack in roasting pan.
4. Roast uncovered at 325°F 3 hours. Remove fat from pan as it accumulates during this period. Turn goose breast side up. Roast 1 to 2 hours longer, or until goose tests done. To test for doneness, move leg gently by grasping end of bone; drumstick-thigh joint should move easily. (Protect fingers with paper napkin.) Allow about 25 minutes per pound to estimate total roasting time.
5. To serve, remove skewers and cord. Place goose on heated platter. Remove some of the apples from goose and arrange on the platter. Garnish with the reserved prunes. For an attractive garnish, place cooked prunes on top of cooked apple rings, if desired.

8 servings

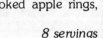

**Roast Beef Filet with Burgundy Sauce
Cheese Sauce for Broccoli; Sherry Baba Ring**

Nudeln *(Buttered Noodles)*

3 quarts water
1 tablespoon salt
3 cups (about 8 ounces) noodles
3 tablespoons butter, melted

1. Heat water and salt to boiling in a large saucepan.
2. Add noodles gradually. Boil rapidly, uncovered, 6 to 10 minutes or until tender. Test tenderness by pressing a piece against side of pan with fork or spoon.
3. Drain noodles by turning them into a colander or large sieve; rinse with hot water. Turn noodles into a warm serving dish. Using a fork, blend butter through noodles.

6 servings

Rotkohl *(Sweet-Sour Red Cabbage)*

1 head (about 2 pounds) red cabbage
Boiling salted water to cover (1 teaspoon salt per quart of water)
⅓ to ½ cup firmly packed brown sugar
¾ teaspoon allspice
4 whole cloves
½ cup vinegar
¼ cup butter

1. Remove and discard wilted outer leaves from cabbage. Rinse, cut into quarters (discarding core), and coarsely shred (about 2 quarts, shredded).
2. Put cabbage into saucepan and add boiling salted water, brown sugar, allspice, and cloves. Cover loosely and boil at a moderate rate 8 to 12 minutes, or until cabbage is just tender.
3. Remove from heat; drain. Add vinegar and butter to cabbage. Toss together lightly to mix.

6 servings

Schaumtorte *(Meringue Torte)*

6 egg whites (about ¾ cup)
2 teaspoons vinegar
1 teaspoon vanilla extract
½ teaspoon almond extract
¼ teaspoon salt
2 cups sugar
1 cup (½ pint) whipping cream, whipped and sweetened

1. Grease bottoms only of two 9-inch round layer cake pans with removable bottoms. (If using solid bottom pans, line with unglazed paper cut to fit bottoms.) Set aside.
2. Beat egg whites until frothy; beat in vinegar, extracts, and salt. Gradually add sugar, continuing to beat until stiff peaks are formed. Turn meringue into prepared pans and spread evenly to edges.
3. Bake at 300°F 40 minutes. Turn off oven, open oven door about 1 or 2 inches, and allow torte layers to dry in oven 30 minutes.
4. Cool torte layers completely on wire racks before removing from pans. (It is likely that top surfaces may become slightly cracked when torte is being removed from pans.)
5. Fill layers with sweetened whipped cream.

One 9-inch torte

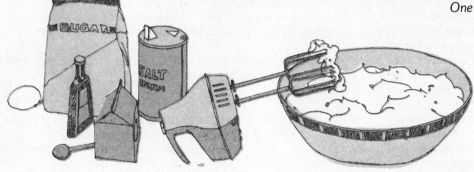

Roast Leg of Lamb with Spicy Wine Sauce;
Peach Wine Mold

ITALIAN DINNER MENU

Course	*Wine*
APPETIZER	
Antipasto (Marinated artichoke hearts, sliced tomatoes, radishes, celery, olives. Thin-sliced meats, such as salami, prosciutto, and capocollo. Sliced hard-cooked eggs. Fish, such as sardines, tuna chunks, and anchovies around capers. Cheese, such as Mozzarella, Provolone, and Gorgonzola)	**Soave**
SOUP	
Minestrone (Vegetable Soup)	**Barolo**
ENTREE	
Saltimbocca (Sliced Veal and Ham with Wine)	**Valpolicella**
Gnocchi in Marinara Sauce (Potato Dumplings in Tomato Sauce)	
Insalata di Asparagi (Asparagus Salad)	
DESSERT	
Zabaglione (Marsala Custard)	**Asti Spumante**
Espresso	

Minestrone

6 cups water
1¼ cups (about ½ pound) pea (navy) beans
¼ pound salt pork
3 tablespoons olive oil
1 small onion, chopped
1 clove garlic, chopped
2 stalks celery
2 small carrots, scraped
1 medium-size potato
¼ head cabbage
1 tablespoon chopped parsley
½ teaspoon salt
¼ teaspoon pepper

1. Heat water to boiling in a large saucepan.
2. Meanwhile, wash beans thoroughly and discard imperfect beans. Gradually add beans to water so boiling will not stop. Simmer 2 minutes and remove from heat. Set aside to soak 1 hour.
3. Add salt pork to beans; return to heat and simmer 1 hour, stirring once or twice.
4. Heat olive oil in a small skillet; add onion and garlic and brown lightly; set aside.
5. Wash celery and carrots and cut into ½-inch slices and set aside. Wash, pare and dice potato; set aside.
6. Wash cabbage in cold water and remove coarse outer leaves; shred finely.
7. Add all vegetables and onion-garlic mixture to beans with

1 quart hot water
¼ cup packaged precooked rice
½ cup frozen green peas
¼ cup tomato paste
    Grated Parmesan cheese

parsley, salt, and pepper. Pour hot water in slowly and simmer about 1 hour, or until beans are tender.

8. Meanwhile cook rice. About 10 minutes before beans are done add rice and peas.

9. When peas are tender, stir in tomato paste and simmer about 5 minutes. Serve sprinkled with Parmesan cheese.

About 6 servings

Saltimbocca *(Sliced Ham and Veal with Wine)*

4 large, thinly sliced veal cutlets
    Salt and pepper
4 large, very thin slices ham or prosciutto
    Dried sage leaves
    Olive oil
¼ cup (2 ounces) Marsala

1. Place veal slices on a cutting board and pound until very thin with a mallet. Divide each slice into 2 or 3 pieces.

2. Season veal with salt and pepper.

3. Cut ham into pieces the same size as veal.

4. Place a sage leaf on each piece of veal and top with a slice of ham. Secure with a wooden pick.

5. Heat several tablespoons olive oil in skillet; add the meat and sauté slowly until golden brown on both sides. Remove meat to heated platter and keep warm.

6. Scrape residue from bottom of pan; add the Marsala and simmer over low heat several minutes. Pour over meat and serve.

4 servings

Gnocchi in Marinara Sauce

Sauce:
½ cup olive oil
2 medium cloves garlic, sliced
3½ cups (28-ounce can) tomatoes, sieved
1¼ teaspoons salt
1 teaspoon oregano
¼ teaspoon chopped parsley
⅛ teaspoon pepper
Gnocchi:
3 medium (about 1 pound) potatoes, cut in quarters
1¾ cups sifted all-purpose flour
3 quarts water
2 tablespoons grated Parmesan cheese

1. For sauce, heat olive oil in a large skillet; add garlic and cook until browned. Add a mixture of tomatoes, salt, oregano, parsley, and pepper slowly, stirring constantly. Cook rapidly uncovered about 15 minutes, or until thickened. Stir occasionally. If sauce becomes too thick, add ¼ to ½ cup water.

2. For gnocchi, wash, pare, and cook potatoes in boiling salted water to cover. Cook about 20 minutes, or until tender when pierced with a fork. Drain. To dry potatoes, shake pan over low heat.

3. Scald potato masher, food mill, or ricer with boiling water. Mash or rice potatoes; keep hot.

4. Measure flour into a bowl. Make a well in center of flour. Add mashed potatoes. (The mashed potatoes should be added when they are very hot.) Mix well to make a soft, elastic dough. Turn dough onto a lightly floured surface and knead.

5. Break off small pieces of dough and use palm of hand to roll pieces to pencil thickness. Cut into pieces about ¾ inch long. Curl each piece by pressing lightly with the index finger and pulling the finger along the piece of dough toward you. Gnocchi may also be shaped by pressing each piece lightly with a floured fork.

6. Bring water to boiling in a saucepan. Gradually add the gnocchi (cook about one-half the gnocchi at one time). Boil rapidly uncovered about 8 to 10 minutes, or until gnocchi are tender and come to the surface. Test tenderness by pressing against side of pan with fork or spoon. Drain by pouring into a colander or large sieve.

7. Mix gnocchi with 2 cups Marinara Sauce and Parmesan cheese. Top with remaining sauce. Serve immediately.

About 6 servings

Insalata di Asparagi (Asparagus Salad)

1 **pound asparagus**
3 **tablespoons olive oil**
3 **tablespoons lemon juice**
1 **medium clove garlic, sliced**
   thin
¼ **teaspoon salt**
⅛ **teaspoon pepper**

1. Prepare and cook asparagus just until tender. Drain and chill in refrigerator.
2. When thoroughly chilled, sprinkle mixture of olive oil, lemon juice, garlic, salt, and pepper over asparagus.

About 3 servings

Zabaglione (Marsala Custard)

6 **egg yolks**
½ **cup sugar**
⅛ **teaspoon salt**
1 **cup Marsala**

1. In a bowl, beat egg yolks until lemon colored with sugar and salt. Stir in Marsala wine.
2. Cook in double boiler over simmering water. Beat constantly with rotary beater until mixture foams up and thickens.
3. Turn into sherbet glasses and chill until serving time.

About 6 servings

SPANISH LUNCHEON MENU

Course	*Wine*
APPETIZER	
Tapas: Huevos Rellenos (Stuffed Eggs), olives, cheese cubes	**Sangria**
ENTREE	
Paella (Shellfish, Chicken, Vegetable, and Rice Stew) Crusty Rolls	**Blanco Seco (Dry White Wine)**
DESSERT	
Islas Flotantes (Floating Island) Café	**Cream Sherry**

Sangria

⅔ **cup lemon juice**
¼ **cup orange juice**
½ **cup sugar**
1 **bottle (4/5 quart) dry red wine**

1. Combine juices and sugar; stir until sugar is dissolved.
2. Pour wine into a pitcher half filled with ice cubes or crushed ice. Add mixture of juices and stir until blended. The proportion of juice mixture to wine should be 1 to 3.

About 8 servings

Islas Flotantes *(Floating Island)*

Soft Custard:
- ¼ cup sugar
- ⅛ teaspoon salt
- 2 eggs, slightly beaten
- 2 egg yolks, slightly beaten
- 2 cups milk, scalded
- 2 teaspoons vanilla extract

Poached Meringues:
- 2 cups milk or water
- 2 egg whites
- ⅛ teaspoon salt
- ¼ teaspoon vanilla extract
- ¼ cup sugar

1. For soft custard, add sugar and salt to beaten eggs and and egg yolks and beat just until blended. Stirring constantly, gradually add scalded milk.
2. Strain mixture into a double-boiler top and cook, stirring constantly, over simmering water until custard coats a metal spoon.
3. Remove from heat and cool to lukewarm over cold water. Stir in extract. Chill.
4. For poached meringues, scald milk or heat water to boiling in a large heavy skillet or saucepan.
5. Beat egg whites, salt, and extract until frothy; add sugar gradually, beating constantly until stiff peaks are formed.
6. Drop egg white mixture by tablespoonfuls, forming 8 mounds, onto scalding milk or boiling water. Cook, uncovered over low heat about 5 minutes, or until "set."
7. Remove meringues with a slotted spoon to waxed or absorbent paper.
8. To serve, put poached meringues, "floating islands," onto chilled custard. If desired, top each meringue with a strawberry and accompany with additional strawberries.

4 servings

Paella

- 1 cup olive oil
- 1 broiler-fryer chicken (2 pounds), cut in serving-sized pieces
- ½ cup diced boiled ham or smoky sausage
- 1 tablespoon finely chopped onion
- 2 cloves garlic, minced
- 2 ripe tomatoes, peeled and coarsely chopped
- 1½ pounds fresh shrimp, shelled and deveined
- 12 small clams in shells, shells scrubbed
- 1½ teaspoons salt
- 2 cups uncooked rice
- 4 cups hot water
- 1 cup fresh or frozen green peas
- ¼ cup coarsely chopped parsley
  Few shreds saffron
- 1 rock lobster tail cooked and meat cut in pieces or 1 package frozen crab meat, thawed, drained, and bony tissue removed
- 1 can or jar (7 ounces) whole pimentos

1. Heat oil in paellera or large skillet. Add chicken and ham and cook about 10 minutes, turning chicken to brown on all sides.
2. Add onion and garlic and cook 2 minutes; add tomatoes, shrimp, clams, and salt; cover and cook 5 to 10 minutes, or until clam shells open. Remove clams and keep warm.
3. Stir rice into mixture. Add water, peas, parsley, and saffron. Cover and cook 25 minutes, or until rice is just tender, stirring occasionally.
4. Mix in the lobster or crab meat, half of the pimento, and the clams in shells; heat until very hot. Serve garnished with the remaining pimento.

8 to 10 servings

GREEK DINNER MENU

Course	*Wine*
APPETIZER	
Tyropitas (Cheese Appetizer Pies; see page 25)	**Ouzo and Soda or Oinos lefkos (Dry White Wine)**
Dolmadakia (Tiny Stuffed Vine Leaves)	
SOUP	
Soupa Avgolemono (Egg-Lemon Soup)	
MEAT	
Souvlakia (Marinated Lamb Cubes Broiled on Skewers)	**Oinos erythros (Dry Red Wine) or Roditis (Rosé)**
Phasolakia Phreska (Buttered Green Beans)	
Salata (Tossed Greens with Black Olives and Crumbled Feta Cheese with Oil and Vinegar Dressing)	
DESSERT	
Glaso Portokali (Glazed Oranges) or Baklava	**Mavrodaphne (Sweet Red Wine) or Moschato (Muscatel)**
Turkish-Style Coffee (available in specialty shops)	

Dolmadakia (Tiny Stuffed Vine Leaves)

1 **jar (8 ounces) grape leaves**
   Cooking oil
1 **medium onion, chopped**
3 **stalks celery, chopped**
3 **tablespoons chopped parsley**
1 **tablespoon chopped green pepper**
1 **pound ground beef round or chuck**
½ **cup rice, cooked**
1½ **teaspoons salt**
½ **teaspoon paprika**

1. Boil grape leaves in large kettle for 5 minutes to remove the brine. Spread out on paper towels to drain. If stems are on the leaves, clip them off.
2. In small amount of cooking oil, sauté the chopped onion, celery, parsley, and green pepper until tender but not brown.
3. Combine the cooked vegetables, meat, cooked rice, and seasonings in mixing bowl.
4. Lay each grape leaf out flat, vein side up, and place 1 teaspoon of meat mixture at center. Bring edges of leaves over meat and roll up to form compact packet about 1½ inches wide.
5. Place each stuffed leaf, folded side down, in a large baking dish; cover dish.

½ teaspoon sage
¼ teaspoon thyme
¼ teaspoon pepper
Lemon Sauce:
¼ pound butter
2 egg yolks
¼ teaspoon salt
1 tablespoon lemon juice

6. Bake at 350°F 1 hour.
7. While leaves are baking, prepare Lemon Sauce.
8. For Lemon Sauce, melt butter in small pan. Transfer about 1 tablespoon of this to small skillet and stir in egg yolks until the mixture is smooth. Over low heat add remaining melted butter and salt to the egg mixture, stirring rapidly until the sauce thickens. Remove from heat and stir in lemon juice.
9. At serving time, pour the sauce over the stuffed grape leaves.

About 3 dozen appetizers

Note: Bake any remaining meat mixture separately in small baking pan.

Souvlakia *(Marinated Lamb Cubes Broiled on Skewers)*

1½ pounds lamb (leg, loin, or shoulder), boneless, cut in 1½-inch cubes
½ cup vegetable oil
1 tablespoon lemon juice
2 teaspoons sugar
½ teaspoon salt
½ teaspoon paprika
¼ teaspoon dry mustard
⅛ teaspoon ground black pepper
¼ teaspoon Worcestershire sauce
1 clove garlic, cut in halves
6 small whole cooked potatoes
6 small whole cooked onions
Butter or margarine, melted
6 plum tomatoes

1. Put lamb cubes into a shallow dish. Combine oil, lemon juice, sugar, salt, paprika, dry mustard, pepper, Worcestershire sauce, and garlic. Pour over meat. Cover and marinate at least 1 hour in refrigerator, turning pieces occasionally. Drain.
2. Alternately thread lamb cubes, potatoes, and onions on 6 skewers. Brush pieces with melted butter.
3. Broil 3 to 4 inches from heat about 15 minutes, or until lamb is desired degree of doneness; turn frequently and brush with melted butter. Shortly before kabobs are done, impale tomatoes on ends of skewers.

6 servings

Soupa Avgolemono *(Egg-Lemon Soup)*

1 lemon
6 chicken bouillon cubes
½ teaspoon salt
2 quarts boiling water
½ cup uncooked long grain rice
4 egg yolks, fork beaten
1 cup heavy cream
2 to 3 tablespoons butter or margarine

1. Pare thin narrow strips of lemon peel. Juice the lemon and measure 4 to 6 tablespoons; set aside.
2. Add the lemon peel, bouillon cubes, and salt to the boiling water in a large saucepot. Stir the rice into the boiling mixture; cover and cook over low heat 20 to 25 minutes, or until rice is soft.
3. Blend the egg yolks, cream, and ½ cup hot broth; stir into soup. Cook and stir over medium heat about 5 minutes. Remove from heat; stir in the reserved lemon juice.
4. Before serving, put the butter into a hot tureen and pour in the soup. Or put butter (about a quarter pat for each serving) into individual soup bowls before ladling the soup. Grind black pepper over surface.

About 3 quarts soup

Glaso Portokali (Glazed Oranges)

6 oranges
Boiling water
2¼ cups (1 pound) sugar
2¼ cups water
Yellow or orange food coloring

1. Pare off the outer colored portions of the orange skins. Cut the peel into tiny slivers.
2. Pour just enough boiling water over the peel to cover. Let stand 10 minutes and drain.
3. Meanwhile, cut off and discard all the white underskin from oranges.
4. Prepare a sugar syrup with the sugar and 2¼ cups water; boil for 10 minutes.
5. Tint with a few drops coloring.
6. Pour boiling syrup over oranges; let stand about 15 minutes.
7. Return syrup to saucepan and boil 15 minutes.
8. Stir in the strips of peel and pour over oranges; cool. Stack oranges pyramid fashion in a serving dish and pour syrup over them to glaze.

6 servings

Baklava

6 cups sugar
3 cups water
1 tablespoon lemon juice
1 pound butter
1 pound pecans
1 pound walnuts
10 zwieback
1 teaspoon cinnamon
3 tablespoons sugar
1 pound filo (phyllo) pastry or strudel leaves—available at specialty shops

1. In saucepan, combine sugar, water, and lemon juice and cook, stirring until sugar is dissolved. Boil 5 minutes and set syrup aside to cool.
2. Melt butter.
3. Chop pecans, walnuts, and zwieback, so there is a mixture of large and small pieces. Add cinnamon and sugar to nut mixture and stir.
4. Remove filo from package, unfold and place on waxed paper and cover with second sheet of waxed paper and a slightly damp tea towel so dough does not dry out while you are working. (If towel is too wet, leaves may stick together.)
5. Grease 15½ x 10½ x 2¼-inch pan. Lay a piece of filo on on the bottom of the pan; it should cover the bottom and if too large, crush it to fit. Brush on melted butter. Repeat until there are four leaves layered.
6. Sprinkle just enough nut mixture over filo in pan to cover lightly.
7. Continue to layer 3 filo, buttering each leaf, and a nut layer until pan is filled. End with filo and butter top well.
8. Cut the baklava about ½ inch inside edges of pan to make a neat edge to the servings. Then cut lengthwise at 1½-inch intervals. Cut diagonally across these lengthwise cuts, again at 1½-inch intervals, to form diamonds.
9. Bake at 300°F 1 hour in middle of oven to insure even heat, or until golden brown.
10. Immediately after baklava comes from oven, pour cooled syrup over top slowly. Store overnight before serving. Will keep in refrigerator for 2 to 3 weeks or can be frozen.

About 50 servings

WINE IN COOKING

Just as wine can lift spirits, it can elevate ordinary recipes to the extraordinary. In the recipes that follow, wine is used as an ingredient to bring other flavors together in harmony and to add an extra quality of its own.

Frugal cooks learned long ago that a sensitive use of wine can give luxurious flavor to inexpensive ingredients. Today, many of the recipes that qualify as "gourmet" fare are an outgrowth of their creativity. Less tender (and therefore less expensive) cuts of meat simmered long and lovingly in a seasoned wine sauce have given rise to such classics as Beef Burgundy and Coq au Vin.

But like any other seasoner, wine shouldn't be overworked. One wine-seasoned dish is ample for one menu. Far from overusing wine, however, the American cook is more apt to overlook it. This collection of recipes is designed to make wine a more familiar ingredient in daily meals.

Save leftover wine for cooking, and don't buy inferior wine. Wine is added for flavor, and cooking won't improve a second-best wine.

BEVERAGES

Kir

1 dash crème de cassis
Dry white wine, such as aligoté chablis, chilled

Combine ingredients, stir, and serve in a well chilled glass.

1 serving

Vermouth Cassis

1 teaspoon crème de cassis
Dry vermouth, chilled

Combine ingredients, stir, and serve in a well chilled glass.

1 serving

Lillet

French vermouth, such as Lillet, chilled
Orange peel

Pour vermouth into well-chilled glass. Garnish with orange peel and serve.

1 serving

Claret Cocktail

1 jigger claret
1 jigger Italian vermouth
¾ teaspoon curaçao
Dash Angostura bitters
Maraschino cherry

Stir well with ice and strain into a cocktail glass. Add a maraschino cherry.

1 serving

Sherry Curaçao Cobbler

3 jiggers sherry
1 teaspoon curaçao.
1 thin piece orange peel
Juice of 1 orange
1 teaspoon sugar

Fill a 10-ounce glass three-fourths full with fine ice. Add sherry, curaçao, orange peel, orange juice, and sugar. Stir well.

1 serving

Port Cobbler

1 teaspoon orange juice
1 teaspoon curaçao
Port
Sugar (optional)

Fill an 8-ounce highball glass two-thirds full with **cracked ice.** Add orange juice and curaçao. Fill with port. Stir until glass is frosted, adding some sugar if you like. Decorate with **fresh fruit.**

1 serving

Cranberry Shrub

2 cups rosé
1 pint bottle cranberry juice cocktail
1 can (6 ounces) frozen pineapple juice concentrate

Combine ingredients and pour over **ice cubes** in a large pitcher. Stir to chill.

4 to 6 servings

Syllabub

2 cups cream
2 cups milk
½ cup sherry
¼ to ½ cup sugar
Few grains salt
Nutmeg

Beat together with a rotary beater until sugar is dissolved and mixture frothy. Serve immediately in punch glasses. Top each serving with a generous sprinkling of nutmeg.

About 8 servings

Champagne Punch

3 jiggers brandy
3 jiggers Cointreau
2 quarts chilled champagne

Place large piece of **ice** in a punch bowl. Add brandy, Cointreau, and chilled champagne. Stir gently and serve.

12 servings

Sherry Eggnog Punch

8 eggs
½ cup sugar
1 bottle (⅘ quart) sherry
1 quart milk
Nutmeg

1. Beat eggs and sugar in mixer until lemon-colored.
2. Stir in sherry and milk; combine well.
3. Serve in tall glasses with ice.
4. Grate nutmeg on each serving.

8 servings

APPETIZERS

Tiny Tomato Toppers

1 package (3 ounces) cream
    cheese, softened
⅓ cup minced cooked chicken
¼ cup finely chopped walnuts
1½ tablespoons finely chopped apple
1½ teaspoons lemon juice
½ teaspoon Worcestershire sauce
½ teaspoon grated onion
2 teaspoons sherry
18 cherry tomatoes, rinsed and
    cut in halves

1. Beat cream cheese in a bowl until fluffy. Add chicken, walnuts, apple, lemon juice, Worcestershire sauce, onion, and sherry; mix thoroughly.
2. Spoon about ½ teaspoon of the chicken mixture onto each tomato half. Chill.

3 dozen appetizers

Brussels Sprouts with Dunking Sauce

2¼ cups dry white wine, such as chablis or sauterne
1 pound fresh Brussels sprouts (or two 10-ounce packages frozen Brussels sprouts)
2 tablespoons butter or margarine
1 tablespoon flour
1 teaspoon salt
½ teaspoon caraway seed
¼ teaspoon cayenne pepper
1 cup milk
1½ cups dairy sour cream

1. Heat the wine in a saucepan until boiling. Add the Brussels sprouts and boil, uncovered, 5 minutes. Cover and boil 5 to 10 minutes, or until just tender. (Cook frozen Brussels sprouts in the wine following package directions.)
2. Meanwhile, stir a mixture of the flour, salt, caraway seed, and cayenne pepper into hot butter in a saucepan. Heat until mixture bubbles. Remove from heat and gradually add the milk, stirring constantly. Return mixture to heat and bring rapidly to boiling, stirring constantly. Boil 1 to 2 minutes, stirring constantly.
3. Reduce heat and stir in the sour cream. Heat thoroughly (do not boil). Keep sauce hot during serving.
4. Drain cooked Brussels sprouts and turn into a serving dish. Spear each sprout and dunk into the sauce.

About 8 servings

Puff Shrimp with Orange Ginger Sauce

Orange Ginger Sauce (see recipe)
Fat for deep frying heated to 375°F
2 pounds medium raw shrimp (20 to 25 per pound)
3 egg yolks
½ cup white wine
¾ cup all-purpose flour
1 teaspoon salt
¼ teaspoon pepper
3 egg whites
Orange Ginger Sauce:
1 cup orange marmalade
2 tablespoons soy sauce
¼ cup sherry
1 piece whole ginger root
1 clove garlic, minced

1. Prepare and cool Orange Ginger Sauce.
2. Fill a deep saucepan or automatic deep fryer one-half to two-thirds full with fat for deep frying; heat slowly to 375°F.
3. Shell and devein raw shrimp and set aside.
4. Beat together in a bowl egg yolks, wine, flour, salt, and pepper until smooth.
5. Beat egg whites until stiff, not dry, peaks are formed. Fold egg whites into egg yolk mixture.
6. Dry shrimp thoroughly and dip into batter, coating well.
7. Deep-fry one layer deep in heated fat 2 to 3 minutes on each side, or until golden brown. Remove from fat with a slotted spoon. Drain on absorbent paper. Be sure temperature of fat is 375°F before frying each layer. Serve shrimp hot accompanied with the Orange Ginger Sauce for dipping.
8. For Orange Ginger Sauce, combine in a saucepan marmalade, soy sauce, sherry, ginger root, and minced garlic. Stir over low heat until mixture bubbles. Remove from heat. Cool. Remove ginger before serving.

40 to 50 appetizers

Oysters Rockefeller

2 tablespoons butter or margarine
2 tablespoons flour
½ teaspoon salt
⅛ teaspoon pepper
1 cup milk (use light cream for richer sauce)
1 egg, well beaten
2 dozen oysters in shells
2 tablespoons sherry
2 tablespoons butter or margarine
1 tablespoon finely chopped onion
1 pound fresh spinach, cooked, drained, and finely chopped
1 tablespoon minced parsley
½ teaspoon Worcestershire sauce
6 drops Tabasco
¼ teaspoon salt
Few grains ground nutmeg
¼ cup shredded Parmesan cheese

1. For sauce, heat 2 tablespoons butter in a saucepan. Blend in flour, salt, and pepper; heat and stir until bubbly.
2. Gradually add the milk, stirring until smooth. Bring to boiling; cook and stir 1 to 2 minutes longer.
3. Stir the egg into white sauce; set aside.
4. Pour **coarse salt** into a 15×10×1-inch jelly roll pan to a ¼-inch depth. Open oysters and arrange the oysters, in the shells, on the salt; sprinkle ¼ teaspoon sherry over each.
5. Heat 2 tablespoons butter in a heavy skillet. Add the onion and cook until partially tender. Add the chopped spinach, 2 tablespoons of the white sauce, parsley, Worcestershire sauce, and Tabasco to the skillet along with salt and nutmeg; mix thoroughly. Heat 2 to 3 minutes.
6. Spoon spinach mixture over all of the oysters; spoon remaining white sauce over spinach. Sprinkle each oyster with cheese.
7. Bake at 375°F 15 to 20 minutes, or until tops are lightly browned.

4 to 6 servings

Wine-Pickled Mushrooms

1 pound fresh mushrooms, sliced lengthwise
1 cup water
⅔ cup white vinegar
½ cup sugar
1 teaspoon salt
½ teaspoon monosodium glutamate
½ teaspoon celery salt
4 sprigs parsley
2 small stalks celery
1 tablespoon mixed pickling spices
1 bay leaf
6 whole cloves
12 peppercorns
½ teaspoon whole allspice
1 cup dry white wine

1. Prepare mushrooms and set aside in a bowl.
2. Mix remaining ingredients, except wine, in a saucepan; bring rapidly to boiling, reduce heat and simmer 10 minutes.
3. Strain the mixture over mushrooms and stir in the wine.
4. Cover and refrigerate several days before serving.

1 quart pickled mushrooms

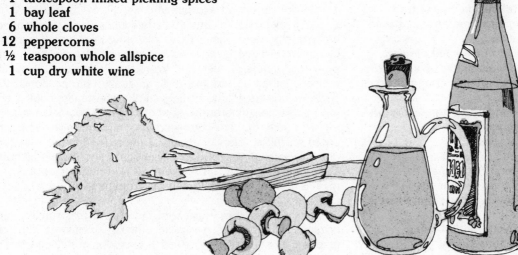

Fabulous Cheese Mousse

¼ cup cold water
1 envelope unflavored gelatin
3¾ ounces (three 1¼-ounce packages) Roquefort cheese
2⅔ ounces (two 1⅓-ounce packages) Camembert cheese
1 egg yolk, slightly beaten
1 tablespoon sherry
1 teaspoon Worcestershire sauce
½ cup chilled whipping cream
1 egg white
Pimento-stuffed olive slices

1. Lightly oil a fancy 1-pint mold with salad or cooking oil (not olive oil); set aside to drain. Chill a small bowl and rotary beater.
2. Pour the cold water into a small cup or custard cup. Sprinkle the gelatin evenly over the water. Let stand about 5 minutes to soften. Dissolve completely by placing cup over very hot water.
3. Force the Roquefort and Camembert cheeses through a fine sieve. Blend in the egg yolk, sherry, and Worcestershire sauce. Stir the dissolved gelatin and add to the cheese mixture, blending thoroughly.
4. Using the chilled bowl and beater, beat whipping cream until it is of medium consistency (piles softly).
5. Using clean beater, beat egg white until rounded peaks are formed. Fold whipped cream and egg white into the cheese mixture. Turn into the mold. Chill until firm.
6. Unmold onto chilled plate and garnish with olive slices. Serve with **crackers.**

One 1-pint mold

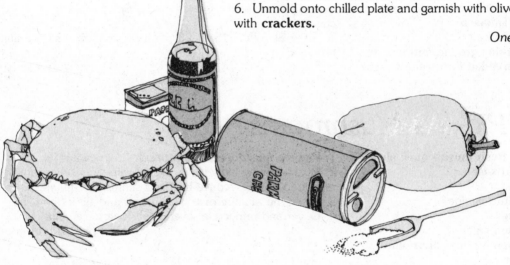

Hot Crab Meat Canapés

2 cups (about 8 ounces) fresh lump crab meat (bony tissue removed)
1 tablespoon chopped pimento
3 tablespoons butter or margarine
1 tablespoon finely chopped green pepper
1 teaspoon finely chopped onion
3 tablespoons flour
½ teaspoon salt
¼ teaspoon dry mustard
Few grains white pepper
Few grains cayenne pepper
½ teaspoon Worcestershire sauce
¾ cup milk
1 egg yolk, slightly beaten
2 tablespoons sherry
5 slices white bread

1. Set out crab meat and pimento.
2. Heat 3 tablespoons butter in a heavy 2-quart saucepan; add green pepper and onion. Cook over low heat 2 to 3 minutes, or until partially tender. Blend in flour, salt, dry mustard, white pepper, cayenne pepper, and Worcestershire sauce. Heat until mixture bubbles. Add the milk gradually, stirring constantly. Bring mixture rapidly to boiling, stirring constantly; cook 1 to 2 minutes longer. Vigorously stir about 3 tablespoons hot mixture into egg yolk. Immediately blend into mixture in saucepan and cook, stirring constantly, about 5 minutes. Add crab meat and pimento to saucepan and mix gently until thoroughly blended. Cook over low heat, stirring gently, 2 to 3 minutes or until crab meat is thoroughly heated. Remove from heat and stir in sherry. Cool.
3. For canapés, trim crust from bread and toast until golden brown. Lightly spread toast with butter. Cover toast with crab meat mixture. Top each slice with 1 teaspoon grated cheese and ½ teaspoon of melted butter. Sprinkle with paprika.

Butter
5 teaspoons grated Parmesan cheese
2½ teaspoons melted butter or margarine
Paprika

4. Cut each toast slice diagonally into 4 triangles and place on a baking sheet.
5. Bake at 425°F 8 to 10 minutes.
6. Place canapés on broiler rack and place rack under broiler with tops of canapés 2 to 3 inches from heat. Broil 1 to 2 minutes.
7. Serve piping hot with **lemon wedges.** If desired, garnish with sprigs of parsley.

20 canapés

Wine-Cheese Canapés

½ cup whipped unsalted butter
4 teaspoons Roquefort cheese
4 toasted bread rounds
2 packages (3 ounces each) cream cheese
2 tablespoons sauterne
Parsley, minced
Pimento-stuffed olive slices
Paprika
Clear Glaze (see recipe)

1. Whip together butter and Roquefort cheese. Spread onto toasted bread rounds.
2. Whip cream cheese with sauterne.
3. Pipe a swirl of the mixture onto each canapé. Roll edges in minced parsley. Top with pimento-stuffed olive slice; sprinkle with paprika.
4. Glaze and chill.

Clear Glaze: Soften **1 envelope unflavored gelatin** in ⅔ **cup cold water** in a bowl. Pour **1 cup boiling water** over softened gelatin and stir until gelatin is dissolved. Chill until slightly thickened. To glaze canapés: Place canapés on wire racks over a large shallow pan. Working quickly, spoon about 2 teaspoons of slightly thickened gelatin over each canapé. (Have ready a bowl of ice and water and a bowl of hot water. The gelatin may have to be set over one or the other during glazing to maintain the proper consistency.) The gelatin should cling slightly to canapés when spooned over them. Any drips may be scooped up and reused.

About 24 canapés

Cocktail Meatballs with Mushroom Curry Sauce

Meatballs:
1 pound ground beef
½ cup fine soft bread crumbs
¼ cup milk
¼ cup sherry
1 egg, slightly beaten
2 tablespoons grated onion
¼ teaspoon ground ginger
1 teaspoon salt
¼ teaspoon pepper
2 tablespoons bacon drippings or other fat
Mushroom Curry Sauce:
1 can (about 10 ounces) condensed cream of mushroom soup
¼ cup sherry
1 teaspoon curry powder

1. For meatballs, mix beef, bread crumbs, milk, wine, egg, onion, ginger, salt, and pepper; shape mixture into little balls, using about one level teaspoon for each.
2. Heat bacon drippings in a large heavy skillet; add a single layer of meatballs and cook, slowly, for about 10 minutes, or until meat is done, shaking pan gently from time to time to cook and brown evenly.
3. When all meat is cooked, spear each with a pick and arrange in hot serving dish.
4. For sauce, combine soup, wine, and curry powder. Heat through and serve piping hot with meatballs.

About 60 meatballs

Avocado Sandwiches on Sour Dough

2 avocados, thinly sliced and salted
¼ cup butter (½ stick), softened
½ teaspoon oregano leaves
¼ teaspoon each chervil, parsley flakes, and grated lemon peel
Dash onion powder
8 slices sour dough or Italian bread, diagonally cut

1. Prepare avocado slices.
2. Cream butter with seasonings. Spread thinly over bread.
3. Top with avocado slices. Serve with white wine.

8 servings

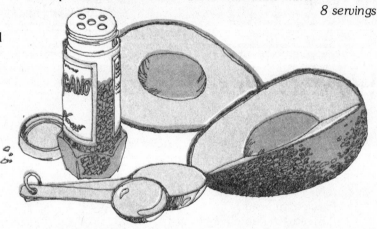

SOUPS

Fresh Fruit Soup

½ pound peaches
½ pound plums
1 quart water
1 cup red wine
1 cup sugar
1 piece (2 inches) stick cinnamon
1 teaspoon cornstarch
2 teaspoons water

1. Rinse peaches and plums, cut into halves, and remove pits.
2. Put fruit into saucepan and add water, wine, sugar, and cinnamon; cover and simmer about 1 hour, or until fruit is very tender. Force the fruit through a fine sieve and return to saucepan.
3. Blend cornstarch and water to make a smooth paste. Stir into the fruit mixture. Bring to boiling. Reduce heat and cook 3 to 5 minutes. Cool. Chill in refrigerator.

3 or 4 servings

Cherry Soup with Wine

3¾ cups water
2 cans (2 to 2½ pounds) frozen sweetened tart red cherries, slightly thawed
½ teaspoon salt
½ cup cold water
¼ cup flour
3 egg yolks, slightly beaten
1 cup dairy sour cream
½ cup sherry

1. Bring water to boiling in a large saucepan. Add cherries and salt. Bring to boiling; simmer, covered, 10 minutes.
2. Pour the cold water into a 1-pint screw-top jar; add flour. Cover jar tightly; shake until blended. Stirring constantly, slowly pour flour mixture into hot cherry mixture; bring to boiling, and cook 2 to 3 minutes.
3. Remove from heat. Gradually add ⅓ cup hot soup to the egg yolks, stirring vigorously; blend into soup. Stirring constantly, cook over low heat 3 to 5 minutes; do not boil. Remove from heat. Gradually add 1 cup hot soup to the sour cream, stirring vigorously. Then blend into remaining soup. Stir in sherry. Serve hot or cold.

8 to 10 servings

Chicken-Avocado Soup

1 can (about 10 ounces) condensed
    cream of chicken soup
1¼ cups water
2 medium ripe avocados
2 to 3 tablespoons lemon juice
1 cup milk
1 thin slice onion
1 stalk celery, cut in several pieces
3 or 4 sprigs parsley, rinsed
½ teaspoon salt
    Few grains pepper
1 to 2 tablespoons sherry

1. Put soup into a 1½-quart saucepan; add water, stirring constantly. Heat to boiling, stirring frequently.
2. Cut avocados into halves; remove pits and peel. Cut 1 avocado half into ½-inch cubes. Put cubes into a small bowl and sprinkle with lemon juice.
3. Put remaining avocado halves into electric blender container with milk, onion, celery, parsley, salt, and pepper. Cover and blend until smooth.
4. Add blended mixture to hot soup and heat quickly to boiling, stirring frequently.
5. Just before serving, add avocado cubes and sherry. Serve at once.

4 or 5 servings

Winter Tomato Soup

½ cup chopped celery
2 tablespoons butter or fresh bacon
    drippings
1 can (16 ounces) stewed tomatoes
1 can (about 10 ounces) condensed
    beef consommé
½ cup dry white wine such as
    sauterne
1 tablespoon instant minced onion
1 tablespoon lemon juice
1 tablespoon cornstarch, blended
    with ½ cup water
⅛ teaspoon curry powder
    Cheese croutons (optional)

1. Sauté the celery in butter or bacon drippings until tender, about 5 minutes.
2. Add tomatoes, consommé, wine, onion, lemon juice, cornstarch blended with water, and curry powder; blend well. Simmer 15 to 20 minutes, stirring occasionally.
3. Garnish with cheese croutons, if desired.

6 servings

Parsley Soup

2 tablespoons chopped onion
2 tablespoons butter
1½ cups chopped parsley (no stems)
2 cups strong chicken stock
½ cup sauterne or other white wine
1 teaspoon salt
3 to 4 drops Tabasco
2 cups half-and-half or cream
    Chopped parsley for garnish

1. Cook onion in butter 2 minutes. Add chopped parsley and cook 3 minutes longer, stirring constantly.
2. Pour in chicken stock, cover, and simmer for 10 minutes.
3. Add wine, salt, and Tabasco, and purée the soup in an electric blender.
4. To serve, stir in half-and-half and heat through. Garnish hot soup with chopped parsley.

4 to 6 servings

Pinto Bean Soup

3 quarts water
1 pound dried pinto beans, washed
1½ teaspoons salt
½ pound boneless lean beef, cut in cubes
¼ cup butter or margarine
1 carrot, diced
1 medium onion, chopped
3 whole cloves
¼ teaspoon mace
¼ cup sherry
3 hard-cooked eggs, sliced
1 lemon, thinly sliced
Paprika

1. Bring water to boiling in a large saucepot or kettle; add beans, bring to boiling and boil 2 minutes. Cover; remove from heat. Allow to stand about 1 hour.
2. Mix salt, beef, butter, carrot, onion, cloves, and mace into undrained beans. Cover and simmer about 2 hours, or until beans are tender.
3. Remove and reserve meat. Discard cloves. Force beans through a food mill or sieve. Return beans and liquid to saucepot; mix in cooked meat and sherry. Heat thoroughly.
4. Turn soup into a tureen. Top with the egg and lemon slices. Sprinkle with paprika.

About 8 servings

Cucumber Soup

½ cup chopped onion
½ cup sliced carrot
4 cups chopped celery (with leaves)
1 tablespoon butter
3 cucumbers, pared and diced
¼ teaspoon thyme
½ teaspoon tarragon leaves, crushed
6 cups chicken broth
2 eggs, slightly beaten
1 cup heavy cream
2 tablespoons dry sherry
1 teaspoon lemon juice
Paprika
Toasted sesame seed

1. In a kettle, cook onion, carrot, and celery with butter until vegetables are soft, about 5 minutes.
2. Add cucumber, thyme, tarragon, and chicken broth; cover and cook 10 minutes. Cool slightly.
3. Pour half of mixture into an electric blender container; blend until smooth. Repeat with remaining half. Pour purée back into kettle; heat thoroughly.
4. Blend beaten eggs with cream. Slowly stir in about ½ cup of hot purée, then stir into remaining hot purée. Heat 5 minutes, stirring constantly. Blend in sherry and lemon juice.
5. Serve sprinkled with paprika and toasted sesame seed.

About 2 quarts soup

Crab Bisque

1 cup crab meat
½ cup sherry
1 can (about 10 ounces) condensed tomato soup
1 can (about 11 ounces) condensed green pea soup
1 soup can half-and-half
½ teaspoon paprika
¼ teaspoon basil

1. Put crab meat into a bowl, pour sherry over, and let stand 1 hour.
2. Blend the tomato and green pea soups, half-and-half, paprika, and basil. Heat slowly, but do not boil. Add the crab meat. Reheat to boiling point and serve immediately.

About 6 servings

Onion Wine Soup

¼ cup butter or margarine
5 large onions, chopped
5 cups broth or bouillon
½ cup celery leaves
1 large potato, sliced
1 cup dry white wine
1 tablespoon vinegar
2 teaspoons sugar
1 cup light cream
1 tablespoon minced parsley
Salt and pepper

1. Heat butter in a large saucepan; add onion and cook 5 minutes.
2. Add broth, celery leaves, and potato; bring to boiling; simmer, covered, 30 minutes. Sieve the mixture, or purée in an electric blender. Return mixture to saucepan. Blend in wine, vinegar, and sugar. Bring to boiling, reduce heat, and simmer 5 minutes.
3. Stir in cream, parsley, and salt and pepper to taste. Heat thoroughly; do not boil.

6 to 8 servings

Black Mushroom-Wine Soup

⅓ cup butter
¾ cup chopped onion
2 ounces dried black mushrooms, broken in small pieces
½ cup chopped celery
1 clove garlic, crushed
2 bay leaves
10 peppercorns
Few sprigs parsley
2 quarts beef broth
3 tablespoons cornstarch
½ cup cold water
¾ cup dry white wine, such as sauterne
¾ teaspoon Worcestershire sauce
¾ teaspoon monosodium glutamate

1. Heat butter in a heavy 3-quart saucepan. Add onion, mushrooms, celery, garlic, bay leaves, peppercorns, and parsley. Stirring occasionally, cook over medium heat about 10 minutes, or until onion and celery become extremely dark in color. Remove from heat.
2. Stirring constantly, slowly add broth and return to heat. Bring to boiling; reduce heat and simmer, partially covered, about 50 minutes.
3. Shortly before end of cooking period, mix the cornstarch and water thoroughly. Gradually add mixture to soup, stirring constantly. Bring to boiling and cook 3 minutes longer. Remove from heat and strain soup, lightly pressing mushrooms against sieve to extract full mushroom flavor.
4. Just before serving stir in the wine, Worcestershire sauce, and monosodium glutamate.

About 2 quarts soup

Note: 1 pound of fresh mushrooms may be substituted for the dried mushrooms.

MEAT

Pot Roast of Beef with Wine

3- to 4-pound beef pot roast, boneless (rump, chuck, or round)
2 cups red wine
2 medium onions, chopped
3 medium carrots, washed, pared,
   and sliced
1 clove garlic
1 bay leaf
¼ teaspoon pepper
4 sprigs parsley
¼ cup all-purpose flour
2 teaspoons salt
¼ teaspoon pepper
3 tablespoons butter
2 cups red wine
1 cup cold water
¼ cup all-purpose flour

1. Put the meat into a deep bowl. Add wine, onions, carrots, garlic, bay leaf, pepper, and parsley. Cover and put into refrigerator to marinate 12 hours, or overnight; turn meat occasionally. Drain the meat, reserving marinade, and pat meat dry with absorbent paper.
2. Coat meat evenly with a mixture of flour, salt, and pepper.
3. Heat butter in a large saucepot; brown the meat slowly on all sides in the butter. Drain off the fat. Add the marinade and wine. Cover and bring to boiling. Reduce heat and simmer slowly 2½ to 3 hours, or until meat is tender.
4. Remove meat to a warm platter.
5. Strain the cooking liquid. Return the strained liquid to saucepot.
6. Pour water into a screw-top jar and add flour; cover jar tightly and shake until mixture is well blended.
7. Stirring constantly, slowly pour one half of the blended mixture into liquid in saucepot. Bring to boiling. Gradually add only what is needed of the remaining blended mixture for consistency desired. Bring gravy to boiling after each addition. Cook 3 to 5 minutes longer.
8. Serve meat with gravy.

8 to 10 servings

Beef Burgundy

This is a family-size recipe. Increase it for a party, as pictured on the cover.

2 slices bacon
2 pounds beef round tip steak, cut
   in 2-inch cubes
2 tablespoons flour
1 teaspoon seasoned salt
1 package beef stew seasoning
   mix
1 cup burgundy
1 cup water
1 tablespoon tomato paste
12 small boiling onions
4 ounces fresh mushrooms, sliced
   and lightly browned in 1
   tablespoon butter or
   margarine
16 cherry tomatoes, stems
   removed

1. Fry bacon in a Dutch oven; remove bacon. Coat meat cubes with a blend of flour and seasoned salt. Add to fat in Dutch oven and brown thoroughly. Add beef stew seasoning mix, burgundy, water, and tomato paste. Cover and simmer gently 45 minutes.
2. Peel onions and pierce each end with a fork so they will retain their shape when cooked. Add onions to beef mixture and simmer 40 minutes, or until meat and onions are tender. Add mushrooms and cherry tomatoes; simmer 3 minutes. Pour into a serving dish.

6 to 8 servings

Note: If cherry tomatoes are not available, use canned whole peeled tomatoes.

Corned Beef

6-pound beef brisket corned, boneless
2 teaspoons whole cloves
½ cup firmly packed light brown sugar
¼ cup sherry

1. Put the meat into a saucepot and add enough water to cover meat. Cover saucepot tightly and bring water just to boiling over high heat. Reduce heat and simmer about 4 hours, or until meat is almost tender when pierced with a fork.
2. Remove from heat and cool in liquid; refrigerate overnight.
3. Remove meat from liquid and set on rack in roasting pan. Stud with cloves. Put brown sugar over top and press firmly.
4. Roast at 325°F 1½ hours. After roasting 30 minutes, drizzle with sherry.
5. To serve, carve meat into slices.

About 12 servings

Roast Beef Filet with Burgundy Sauce

1 beef loin tenderloin roast, center cut (about 4 pounds)
Salt and pepper
½ cup dry red wine, such as burgundy
Sautéed mushroom caps
Parsley-buttered potatoes
Spiced crab apples

Burgundy Sauce:
½ cup warm water
¼ cup flour
1 cup beef broth
½ cup burgundy

1. Have meatman trim all but a thin layer of fat from meat and roll meat like a rib roast (but without adding fat).
2. Rub meat with salt and pepper and place in shallow roasting pan. Insert meat thermometer into center of thickest portion of roast.
3. Roast in a very hot oven, 450°F, about 45 to 60 minutes until thermometer registers 140°F (rare), basting twice with the wine after meat has cooked for 20 minutes.
4. Remove roast to heated serving platter. Garnish with sautéed mushroom caps, parsley-buttered potatoes, and spiced crab apples. Serve with Burgundy Sauce.
5. For sauce, pour off clear fat from drippings, saving ¼ cup.
6. Pour warm water into roasting pan; stir and scrape up all brown bits; strain.
7. Heat the reserved fat in a skillet; stir in flour. Slowly stir in strained liquid, beef broth, and burgundy. Cook and stir until sauce boils and thickens. Add a few drops of gravy coloring, if desired.

6 to 8 servings

Boulettes of Beef Stroganoff

1 pound ground beef round steak
1 egg, lightly beaten
⅓ cup fine fresh bread crumbs
¼ cup milk
¼ teaspoon grated nutmeg
¼ teaspoon each salt and freshly
    ground pepper
3 tablespoons paprika
¼ cup butter
¼ pound mushrooms, thinly sliced
⅓ cup finely chopped onion
¼ cup dry sherry
2 tablespoons brown sauce or
    canned beef gravy
¼ cup heavy cream
1 cup dairy sour cream
¼ cup finely chopped parsley

1. Put the meat into a mixing bowl and add the egg.
2. Soak the crumbs in milk and add this to the meat. Add the nutmeg, salt, and pepper; mix well with the hands. Shape the mixture into balls about 1½-inches in diameter. There should be about 35 to 40 meatballs.
3. Sprinkle a pan with the paprika and roll the meatballs in it.
4. Heat the butter in a heavy skillet and cook the meatballs, turning gently, until they are nicely browned, about 5 minutes. Sprinkle the mushrooms and onion between and around the meatballs and shake the skillet to distribute the ingredients evenly. Cook about 1 minute and partially cover. Simmer about 5 minutes and add the wine and brown sauce.
5. Stir in the heavy cream. Partially cover and cook over low heat about 15 minutes. Stir in the sour cream and bring just to boiling without cooking. Sprinkle with parsley and serve piping hot with **buttered fine noodles** as an accompaniment.

4 to 6 servings

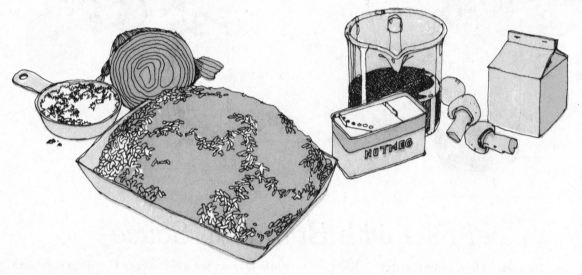

Beef Stroganoff

1½ pounds well-trimmed beef loin
    top sirloin steak, boneless
2 cups sliced mushrooms
3 tablespoons butter
1 shallot, chopped
¼ bay leaf
¾ cup dry sherry
2 tablespoons cornstarch
1 can (about 10 ounces)
    condensed beef broth
½ teaspoon salt
    Pepper to taste
1 cup dairy sour cream
1 tablespoon finely chopped
    parsley

1. Broil steak until rare. Cool thoroughly, then cut into strips.
2. Saute mushrooms in butter. Add shallot, bay leaf, and sherry; boil 5 minutes, until wine is reduced in volume to about half. Remove bay leaf.
3. Stir cornstarch into a little of the broth. Turn remaining broth over mushrooms, add cornstarch mixture, and cook-stir until sauce boils thoroughly and thickens. Add salt and pepper.
4. Just before serving, reheat sauce, then stir in sour cream and parsley and heat until simmering. Add steak strips and heat, but do not boil. Serve as soon as steak is thoroughly heated.

6 servings

Tenderloin Supreme in Mushroom Sauce

1 whole beef loin tenderloin roast
   (4 to 6 pounds)
Mushroom Sauce:
⅓ cup butter
¾ cup sliced mushrooms
¾ cup finely chopped onion
1½ tablespoons flour
¾ teaspoon salt
⅛ teaspoon pepper
⅛ teaspoon thyme
1½ cups beef broth
¾ cup red wine, such as burgundy
1½ teaspoons wine vinegar
1½ tablespoons tomato paste
1½ teaspoons chopped parsley

1. Place tenderloin on rack in roasting pan. Insert roast meat thermometer in center of meat so that tip is slightly more than halfway through meat.
2. Roast, uncovered, at 425°F 45 to 60 minutes. The roast will be rare when meat thermometer registers 140°F.
3. For Mushroom Sauce, heat butter in a skillet. Add mushrooms and cook over medium heat until lightly browned and tender, stirring occasionally. Remove mushrooms with a slotted spoon, allowing butter to drain back into skillet; set aside.
4. Add onion and cook 3 minutes; blend in flour, salt, pepper, and thyme. Heat until mixture bubbles. Remove from heat.
5. Gradually add, stirring constantly, beef broth, wine, and wine vinegar. Cook rapidly until sauce thickens. Blend in the mushrooms, tomato paste, and parsley. Cook about 3 minutes.
6. Serve slices of beef tenderloin with sauce spooned over individual servings.

16 to 24 servings

Roast Leg of Lamb with Spicy Wine Sauce

1 cup dry red wine
¼ cup salad oil
1 onion, coarsely chopped
2 cloves garlic, minced
½ teaspoon Tabasco
2 teaspoons salt
1 lamb leg whole (6 to 8 pounds)
   Parsley

1. Combine wine, oil, onion, garlic, Tabasco, and salt; pour over lamb. Cover and refrigerate 6 hours or overnight, turning occasionally.
2. Place lamb on rack in shallow roasting pan. Roast at 325°F about 25 minutes per pound, or until meat thermometer registers 160° to 170°F (medium); baste occasionally with marinade.
3. Garnish with parsley.

12 to 16 servings

Company Affair Lamb Chops

3 tablespoons butter
3 tablespoons flour
1 cup rich beef stock
¼ cup diced smoked pork loin,
   Canadian style bacon, or lean
   ham
1 tablespoon butter
¼ cup sherry
2 tablespoons minced green pepper
6 slices eggplant, cut ½ inch
   thick; unpeeled
   Olive oil
6 lamb loin chops
6 broiled mushroom caps

1. Melt butter in saucepan; add flour and cook until lightly browned. Gradually add beef stock and cook sauce until smooth and thick.
2. Combine bacon and butter in skillet and fry at least 2 minutes. Add sherry and green pepper and add to sauce.
3. Brush eggplant with olive oil and broil until lightly browned.
4. Broil lamb chops so that they are pink and juicy inside and crisply browned on outside.
5. Pour hot sauce over eggplant slices and place one lamb chop on each slice of eggplant. Garnish with a mushroom cap.

6 servings

Lamb Chops Burgundy

8 lamb loin or rib chops, cut 1½ to
    2 inches thick
½ cup burgundy
¼ cup olive oil
⅔ cup chopped red onion
½ clove garlic, minced
¼ teaspoon salt
3 peppercorns, crushed
½ teaspoon cumin seed, crushed

1. Put lamb chops into a shallow dish.
2. Combine burgundy, olive oil, red onion, garlic, salt, peppercorns, and cumin in a screw-top jar and shake to blend.
3. Pour marinade over meat. Cover and set in refrigerator to marinate about 2 hours, turning chops occasionally.
4. Remove chops from marinade and place on broiler rack. Set under broiler with tops of chops 3 to 5 inches from heat. Broil 18 to 22 minutes, or until meat is done as desired; turn once and brush occasionally with remaining marinade. To test, slit meat near bone and note color of meat.

8 servings

Party Lamb Chops

6 lamb loin chops, about 2 pounds
½ teaspoon salt
⅛ teaspoon pepper
2 tablespoons butter
2 tablespoons prepared mustard
1 can (16 ounces) quartered
    hearts of celery
1 cup tomato juice
½ cup dry white wine, such as
    sauterne
¼ cup finely chopped parsley

1. Sprinkle chops with salt and pepper.
2. Brown chops on both sides in butter in skillet. Spread mustard on chops.
3. Add celery and liquid from can, tomato juice, and wine. Cover and simmer 1 hour over low heat until chops are tender. Place chops on platter and keep warm.
4. Pour pan juices into blender and whirl until smooth, or beat with a rotary beater in small bowl. Pour back into skillet and reheat until bubbly and thick. Spoon over chops. Sprinkle chops with parsley.

6 servings

Lamb Chops with Dill Sauce

3 tablespoons butter
½ cup chopped onion
4 lamb shoulder arm chops, cut ½
    inch thick
2 tablespoons water
1 tablespoon vinegar
1 teaspoon salt
¼ teaspoon pepper
1 bay leaf
2 tablespoons butter or margarine
2 tablespoons flour
¼ teaspoon salt
    Few grains pepper
½ cup beef broth
1 tablespoon chopped fresh dill
½ cup dry white wine, such as
    chablis or sauterne
2 tablespoons vinegar

1. For chops, melt butter in a large heavy skillet with a tight-fitting cover. Add onion to fat and cook slowly, stirring occasionally, about 5 minutes. Remove onion from skillet with slotted spoon to small dish and set aside.
2. Cut through fat about every inch on outside edges of lamb chops. Be careful not to cut through to lean meat. Place chops in skillet; slowly brown both sides.
3. Meanwhile, combine water, vinegar, salt, pepper, and bay leaf; slowly add this mixture to the browned lamb. Return onion to skillet. Cover skillet and simmer 25 to 30 minutes, or until lamb is tender when pierced with a fork. If needed, add small amounts of water as lamb cooks.
4. For sauce, melt butter in small skillet over low heat. Blend flour, salt, and pepper into butter until smooth. Heat mixture until bubbly and lightly browned. Remove skillet from heat. Gradually add a mixture of the broth and fresh dill, stirring constantly.
5. Bring rapidly to boiling, stirring constantly; cook 1 to 2 minutes longer. Remove sauce from heat and gradually add wine and vinegar, stirring constantly. Serve the sauce over lamb chops.

4 servings

Stuffed Veal Steak

4 veal loin top loin chops, 1 inch
   thick (about 1½ pounds)
1 cup dry white wine, such as chablis
½ cup sliced mushrooms
1 green pepper, cut in ½-inch pieces
½ cup butter or margarine
½ cup all-purpose flour
1 egg, fork beaten
½ cup fine dry bread crumbs
½ cup grated Parmesan cheese
4 slices proscuitto (Italian ham)
4 slices (4 ounces) Cheddar cheese

1. Make a cut in the side of each veal chop, cutting almost all the way through. Lay each open and pound flat. Marinate meat for 1 hour in wine.
2. While meat marinates, sauté mushrooms and green pepper in butter for about 10 minutes or until tender. Remove from skillet with slotted spoon, leaving butter in skillet. Set vegetables aside.
3. Dry veal on paper towel. Bread on one side only, dipping first in flour, then in beaten egg, and last in bread crumbs mixed with Parmesan cheese.
4. Lay a slice of proscuitto on one half of unbreaded side of veal. Fold other side over. Panfry for 6 minutes on one side in butter in skillet, adding more butter if needed. Turn veal, and remove skillet from heat.
5. Insert a slice of cheese and ¼ of the mushroom-pepper mixture into the fold of each steak.
6. Return to heat and cook 6 minutes, or until meat is tender.

4 servings

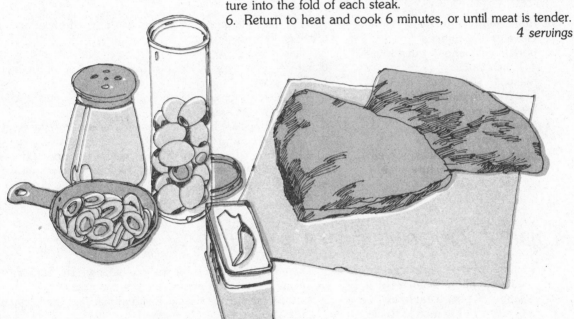

Veal Cutlet in Wine with Olives

1½ pounds veal cutlets, cut about ¼
    inch thick
¼ cup all-purpose flour
1 teaspoon salt
½ teaspoon monosodium
   glutamate
¼ teaspoon pepper
2 to 3 tablespoons butter or
   margarine
⅓ cup marsala
⅓ cup sliced green olives

1. Place meat on flat working surface and pound with meat hammer to increase tenderness. Turn meat and repeat process. Cut into 6 serving-size pieces. Coat with a mixture of flour, salt, monosodium glutamate, and pepper.
2. Heat butter in skillet over low heat. Brown meat over medium heat. Add marsala and green olives. Cover skillet and cook over low heat about 1 hour, or until meat is tender when pierced with a fork.

About 6 servings

Veal in Wine-Mushroom Sauce

1½ pounds thin veal cutlets
1 clove garlic, peeled and cut
1 tablespoon flour
¼ cup butter or margarine
½ pound mushrooms, thinly sliced
½ teaspoon salt
Dash white pepper
½ cup white wine, such as vermouth
1 teaspoon lemon juice (optional)
Snipped parsley

1. Pound meat to ¼-inch thickness. Rub both sides with garlic. Cut veal into 2-inch pieces and sprinkle with flour.
2. Sauté veal, a few pieces at a time, in hot butter in a large skillet, until golden brown on both sides.
3. Return all pieces to skillet. Top with mushrooms and sprinkle with salt and pepper.
4. Add wine and cook, covered, over low heat for 20 minutes, or until fork tender, adding 1 tablespoon or so of water if necessary.
5. To serve, sprinkle with lemon juice, if desired, and parsley.

4 to 6 servings

Neapolitan Pork Chops

2 tablespoons olive oil
1 clove garlic, minced
6 pork loin rib chops, cut about ¾ to 1 inch thick
1 teaspoon salt
½ teaspoon monosodium glutamate
¼ teaspoon pepper
1 pound mushrooms
2 green peppers
½ cup canned tomatoes, sieved
3 tablespoons dry white wine

1. Heat oil in large heavy skillet, add minced garlic and cook until lightly browned.
2. Season pork chops with a mixture of the salt, monosodium glutamate, and pepper. Place in skillet and slowly brown chops on both sides.
3. While chops brown, clean and slice mushrooms and chop green peppers; set aside.
4. When chops are browned, add the mushrooms and peppers. Stir in tomatoes and wine, cover skillet and cook over low heat 1 to 1½ hours, depending on thickness of chops. Add small amounts of water as needed. Test the chops for tenderness by piercing with a fork.

6 servings

Apple-Covered Ham in Claret

2 smoked ham center slices, fully cooked, about ¾ inch thick (about ½ pound each) or 1 large center cut 1½ inches thick
½ teaspoon dry mustard
3 to 4 medium Golden Delicious apples, cored and cut in rings
4 orange slices
¾ cup dry red wine, such as claret
½ cup packed brown sugar
Parsley sprigs

1. Place ham slices in large shallow baking dish. Sprinkle each slice with ¼ teaspoon mustard.
2. Cut unpared apple rings in half and place around outer edge of ham, slightly overlapping slices.
3. Place two orange slices in center of each ham slice.
4. Pour wine over top of ham and fruit. Then sprinkle entire dish with brown sugar.
5. Cover; cook in a 350°F oven 45 minutes. Serve on platter or from baking dish, and garnish with parsley.

6 to 8 servings

FISH

Curried Prawns

1 pound large prawns, peeled
    and deveined
2 tablespoons butter
1 tablespoon chopped scallions
1 tablespoon flour
1 teaspoon curry powder
¼ cup sauterne
2 cups cream
    Hot rice

1. Sauté prawns in heated butter in skillet 2 to 3 minutes; add scallions and sauté 3 to 4 minutes longer. Sprinkle with a mixture of flour and curry powder. Cook and stir about 3 minutes.
2. Stir in the wine and cream and simmer mixture 10 minutes, stirring occasionally. Transfer prawns to a chafing dish using a slotted spoon.
3. Continue cooking the sauce over low heat to desired consistency. Add seasoning, if desired, and pour over the prawns. Serve with hot rice.

2 servings

Broiled Salmon

6 salmon steaks, cut ½ inch thick
1 cup sauterne
½ cup vegetable oil
2 tablespoons wine vinegar
2 teaspoons soy sauce
2 tablespoons chopped green onion
    Seasoned salt
    Green onion, chopped (optional)
    Pimento strips (optional)

1. Put salmon steaks into a large shallow dish. Mix sauterne, oil, wine vinegar, soy sauce, and green onion; pour over salmon. Marinate in refrigerator several hours or overnight, turning occasionally.
2. To broil, remove steaks from marinade and place on broiler rack. Set under broiler with top 6 inches from heat. Broil about 5 minutes on each side, brushing generously with marinade several times. About 2 minutes before removing from broiler, sprinkle each steak lightly with seasoned salt and, if desired, top with green onion and pimento. Serve at once.

6 servings

Fresh Vegetables and Shrimp en Brochette

1¾ pounds fresh shrimp (23 to 25
    uncooked shrimp), washed,
    peeled, and deveined
1 pound fresh mushrooms (about
    12 mushrooms) with stem
    ends removed
2 medium tomatoes, quartered
2 medium green peppers, seeded
    and cut in 1½-inch cubes
2 medium onions, peeled and
    quartered
¾ cup oil
½ cup dry white wine or sherry
¼ cup chopped parsley
1 teaspoon salt
¼ teaspoon pepper

1. Combine shrimp and vegetables in a bowl.
2. Prepare marinade by combining oil, wine, parsley, salt, and pepper. Pour over shrimp and vegetables. Allow to marinate for 3 hours.
3. String shrimp on skewers alternately with vegetables. Broil about 3 inches from heat until shrimp are browned and flake easily; about 4 minutes on one side, 3 minutes on the other.

4 to 6 servings

Fish Stew with Red Wine

2 pounds fish
2 cups red wine
1 carrot, sliced
1 onion, minced
2 cloves garlic, cut in halves
1 teaspoon salt
¼ teaspoon pepper
Herb Bouquet
3 tablespoons brandy
3 tablespoons melted butter
2 tablespoons all-purpose flour

1. Set out a deep heavy skillet with a tight-fitting cover.
2. Clean, wash, dry, and cut fish into thick slices. Put fish into skillet and add wine, carrot, onion, garlic, salt, pepper, and Herb Bouquet; bring to boiling.
3. Heat brandy in a small saucepan. Ignite brandy and immediately pour over the fish. When the flame has burned out, cover the pan. Cook fish slowly 15 to 20 minutes, or until the fish flakes when pierced with a fork. Remove fish to a warm serving dish. Keep hot. Strain and reserve cooking liquid.
4. Blend thoroughly in same skillet butter and flour. Cook over low heat until mixture bubbles. Remove from heat; gradually stir in cooking liquid. Cook rapidly; stir constantly until sauce thickens. Boil 1 to 2 minutes longer. Pour sauce over the fish.
5. Serve with **garlic croutons.** Garnish with **tiny cooked onions, sautéed mushrooms,** or **cooked shrimp.**

4 servings

Herb Bouquet: Tie together neatly **3 or 4 sprigs of parsley, 1 sprig thyme,** and **½ bay leaf.** If dry herbs are used, enclose in fine cheesecloth bag.

Mussels Cooked in Wine Sauce

2 quarts mussels
2 cups dry white wine such as chablis
1 cup finely chopped shallots
½ cup finely chopped parsley
⅓ cup unsalted butter
Freshly ground white pepper
Juice of ½ lemon
Salt
Hollandaise Sauce:
2 egg yolks
2 tablespoons cream

1. Scrub mussels under running water and trim off the beards.
2. Pour wine over mussels in a saucepot; add shallots, parsley, butter, and white pepper to taste. Cover tightly and cook over high heat about 2 minutes; stir the mixture and cook, covered, 2 minutes longer, or until mussel shells open.
3. Remove the mussels from saucepot; remove and discard top shells, placing the filled bottom shells in a serving dish. Keep warm.
4. Cook the pan juice over high heat to reduce the amount by one half. Remove from heat. Add lemon juice, salt, and white pepper to taste.
5. For hollandaise sauce, in the top of a double boiler, beat egg

¼ teaspoon salt
Few grains cayenne pepper
2 tablespoons lemon juice or
tarragon vinegar
½ cup butter

yolks, cream, salt, and cayenne pepper until thick with a whisk beater. Set over hot (not boiling) water. (Bottom of double-boiler top should not touch water.)

6. Add the lemon juice gradually, while beating constantly. Cook, beating constantly with the whisk beater, until sauce is the consistency of thick cream. Remove double boiler from heat, leaving top in place.

7. Beating constantly, add the butter, ½ teaspoon at a time. Beat with whisk beater until butter is melted and thoroughly blended in. Mix with wine sauce.

8. Pour the sauce over the mussels and serve immediately.

4 servings

Scallops Baked in Shells

2 cups dry white wine
Herb Bouquet
2 pounds (1 quart) scallops
½ teaspoon salt
½ pound mushrooms
6 shallots or ¼ cup minced onions
1 tablespoon minced parsley
3 tablespoons butter
2 tablespoons water
1 teaspoon lemon juice
¼ cup melted butter
¼ cup all-purpose flour
2 egg yolks, slightly beaten
¼ cup heavy cream
⅓ cup buttered dry bread crumbs

1. Butter 6 baking shells or ramekins.
2. Heat wine in a saucepan with Herb Bouquet.
3. Wash scallops in cold water and drain.
4. Add scallops and salt to wine, cover and simmer about 10 minutes, or until tender. Remove Herb Bouquet, drain scallops, and reserve the liquid. Cut scallops into fine pieces and set aside.
5. Clean and chop mushrooms.
6. Add mushrooms, shallots, parsley, butter, water, and lemon juice to a saucepan; cover and simmer 5 to 10 minutes. Strain liquid into seasoned wine. Add vegetable mixture to scallops. Set aside.
7. Make a roux by blending butter and flour in a saucepan. Cook over low heat until mixture bubbles. Remove from heat and gradually stir in wine and vegetable liquid. Return to heat and bring rapidly to boiling, stirring constantly; cook 1 to 2 minutes longer.
8. Remove sauce from heat and add egg yolks and cream gradually, stirring vigorously. Then stir in the scallop mixture.
9. Fill shells or ramekins, piling high in center. Sprinkle with about ⅓ cup of buttered bread crumbs.
10. To brown, set shells on a baking sheet and place in oven at 450°F 8 to 10 minutes, or place under broiler 3 to 4 minutes from heat to top of the creamed mixture. Serve when browned.

6 servings

Herb Bouquet: Tie neatly together **3 or 4 sprigs of parsley, 1 sprig thyme,** and **½ bay leaf.** If dry herbs are used, enclose in fine cheesecloth bag.

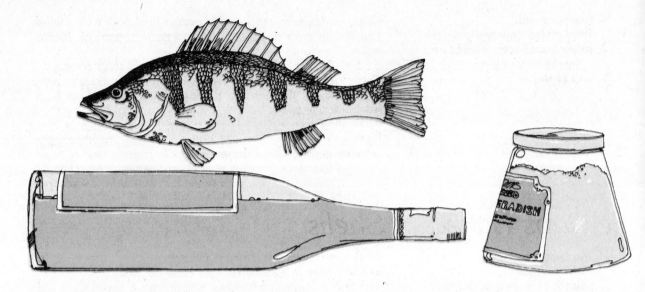

Poached Fish with Horseradish Sauce

1½ **pounds fish fillets, such as perch or bass**
   Boiling water (enough to just cover fish)
½ **cup dry white wine**
1 **small onion, chopped**
2 **tablespoons chopped parsley**
1 **teaspoon salt**
⅛ **teaspoon pepper**

Horseradish Sauce:
1 **cup dairy sour cream**
2 **to 3 tablespoons prepared horseradish**
2 **tablespoons grated lemon peel**

1. For poached fish, tie fish loosely in cheesecloth to prevent breaking and place in a skillet. Add boiling water, wine, onion, parsley, salt, and pepper. Cover skillet and simmer about 10 minutes, or until fish flakes (can be separated with a fork into thin, layer-like pieces). Meanwhile, prepare sauce.
2. For sauce, blend well sour cream, horseradish, and lemon peel. Pour sauce into serving dish; set aside.
3. Drain fish; remove cheesecloth. Place fish on warm platter. Serve with sauce.

4 servings

Shrimp à la King

2 **cups white wine**
2 **shallots, minced, or ¼ cup minced onion**
1 **cup oyster liquor, fish stock, or chicken broth**
1½ **pounds fresh shrimp, peeled and deveined**
2 **tablespoons flour**
2 **tablespoons butter**
   Juice of ¼ lemon (about 2 teaspoons)
½ **cup light cream**
2 **egg yolks, well beaten**
   Toast points
   Parsley

1. Combine wine, shallots, and oyster liquor in a saucepan; bring to boiling and add shrimp. Simmer 15 minutes. Drain and reserve ¾ cup stock.
2. Meanwhile, stir flour into melted butter in a saucepan, making a roux. Blend in reserved stock; cook and stir until mixture thickens. Add shrimp and cook over low heat. Stir in lemon juice.
3. Add cream to beaten yolks. Mix well and add hot shrimp mixture, stirring constantly. Serve on toast points and garnish with parsley.

4 to 6 servings

Lobster Newburg/Crab Meat Newburg

2 cups cooked lobster meat
¼ cup butter
2 cups cream
¾ teaspoon salt
⅛ teaspoon pepper
⅛ teaspoon nutmeg
4 egg yolks, slightly beaten
2 tablespoons sherry
Toast points or cooked rice

1. Cut lobster meat into 1-inch pieces and set aside.
2. Melt butter in the top of a double boiler. Blend in cream, salt, pepper, and nutmeg; bring just to boiling. Stir in lobster and cook over low heat until lobster is thoroughly heated.
3. Vigorously stir about 3 tablespoons of hot mixture into egg yolks. Immediately blend into hot mixture. Place over simmering water and cook 3 to 5 minutes, or just until mixture thickens. Stir slowly to keep mixture cooking evenly. (Do not overcook as sauce will curdle.)
4. Remove immediately from heat and blend in sherry. Serve on toast points or cooked rice.

About 6 servings

Crab Meat Newburg: Follow recipe for Lobster Newburg substituting **2 cups cooked crab meat** for the lobster. Remove and discard bony tissue from meat.

Oysters Royale

6 tablespoons butter
½ clove garlic, minced
½ cup diced celery
½ cup diced green pepper
6 or 7 tablespoons flour
½ teaspoon salt
¼ teaspoon white pepper
Few grains cayenne pepper
2 cups cream
1½ pints oysters, drained; reserve
⅓ cup liquor (see Note)
1 teaspoon prepared mustard
2 ounces Gruyère cheese, cut in
pieces
¼ cup dry sherry

1. Heat butter in a saucepan. Add garlic, celery, and green pepper; cook about 5 minutes, or until vegetables are crisp-tender. Remove vegetables with a slotted spoon and set aside.
2. Blend a mixture of flour, salt, and peppers into the butter in saucepan; heat until mixture bubbles. Remove from heat; add cream and reserved oyster liquor gradually, stirring constantly. Continue stirring, bring to boiling, and boil 1 to 2 minutes. Remove from heat.
3. Blend in the mustard and cheese, stirring until cheese is melted. Mix in the wine, vegetables, and oysters. Bring just to boiling and remove from heat. (Edges of oysters should just begin to curl.) Turn into blazer pan of chafing dish and set over simmering water.
4. Accompany with a basket of **toasted buttered 3½-inch bread rounds** sprinkled lightly with **ground nutmeg**.

10 to 12 servings

Note: The amount of liquor in a pint of oysters varies. This recipe was tested using ⅓ cup, but slightly less will not affect the recipe.

POULTRY

Brunswick Stew

1 chicken (about 4 pounds),
    disjointed
¼ cup cooking oil
1 cup coarsely chopped onion
¼ pound salt pork, chopped
4 tomatoes, peeled and quartered
2 cups boiling water
1 cup sherry
1 bay leaf
1 teaspoon Worcestershire sauce
1½ cups fresh lima or butter beans
½ cups sliced fresh okra
1½ cups fresh bread crumbs
2 tablespoons butter
    Salt to taste

1. Sauté chicken in cooking oil until golden; remove chicken. Brown onion and salt pork in the same fat.
2. Put chicken, salt pork, onion, tomatoes, boiling water, sherry, bay leaf, and Worcestershire sauce into Dutch oven or saucepot. Cover and simmer 2 hours, or until chicken is tender.
3. After 1 hour, remove bay leaf; add beans and cook about 15 minutes. Add sliced okra; continue cooking about 15 minutes.
4. Sauté fresh bread crumbs in butter; stir into stew. Add salt to taste before serving.

8 servings

Chicken Breasts with Noodles

8 whole chicken breasts, flattened
    Salt and pepper to taste
    Dash of crushed marjoram
    Butter to cover skillet
3 pounds fresh mushrooms
½ pound butter
12 ounces noodles
2 tablespoons butter
2 cups Medium White Sauce
    (see recipe)
1 cup cold milk
1 cup chicken broth
    Hollandaise Sauce (see recipe)
½ cup dry white wine
    Parmesan cheese, grated

1. Season chicken breasts with salt, pepper, and marjoram. Sauté in butter until breasts are fully cooked.
2. While chicken is cooking, wash mushrooms and cut into small pieces, then sauté in ½ pound butter.
3. Cook noodles until done; drain and work 2 tablespoons of butter gently into the noodles.
4. Make white sauce; add to it the cold milk and chicken broth. Cook mixture until thickened. Reserve while making hollandaise sauce.
5. Carefully blend hollandaise with white sauce mixture; stir in wine.
6. Butter a small roasting pan; place noodles in the bottom, add the mushrooms, and place chicken breasts on top of the mushrooms. Pour the sauce over all. Heat thoroughly in a 325°F oven about 45 minutes.
7. Remove from oven, sprinkle with grated Parmesan cheese and place under broiler to brown.

8 servings

Medium White Sauce: Melt **¼ cup butter or margarine** in a saucepan. Blend in **¼ cup flour, 1 teaspoon salt,** and **¼ teaspoon pepper.** Cook and stir until bubbly. Gradually add **2 cups milk,** stirring until smooth. Bring to boiling; cook and stir 1 to 2 minutes longer.

About 2 cups sauce

Hollandaise Sauce: Beat **4 egg yolks** in the top of a double boiler, then beat in **½ cup cream.** Cook and stir over **hot water** until slightly thickened. Blend in **2 tablespoons lemon juice.** Cut in **4 tablespoons cold butter,** a tablespoon at a time. Sauce will thicken.

About 1 cup sauce

Chicken Curry with Rice

⅔ cup butter or margarine
6 tablespoons chopped onion
6 tablespoons chopped celery
6 tablespoons chopped green apple
24 peppercorns
2 bay leaves
⅔ cup all-purpose flour
5 teaspoons curry powder
1 teaspoon monosodium glutamate
½ teaspoon sugar
¼ teaspoon nutmeg
5 cups milk
4 teaspoons lemon juice
1 teaspoon Worcestershire sauce
½ cup cream
¼ cup sherry
½ teaspoon Worcestershire sauce
6 cups cubed cooked chicken
Hot cooked rice

1. Heat butter in a heavy 3-quart saucepan over low heat. Add onion, celery, apple, peppercorns, and bay leaves, and cook over medium heat until lightly browned, occasionally moving and turning with a spoon.
2. Blend in flour, curry powder, monosodium glutamate, sugar, and nutmeg; heat until mixture bubbles.
3. Remove from heat and add milk gradually, stirring constantly.
4. Return to heat and bring rapidly to boiling. Stirring constantly, cook until mixture thickens; cook 1 to 2 minutes longer.
5. Remove from heat; add lemon juice and 1 teaspoon Worcestershire sauce. Strain mixture through a fine sieve, pressing vegetables against sieve to extract all sauce. Set sauce aside.
6. Reheat the curry sauce and blend in cream, sherry, and ½ teaspoon Worcestershire sauce; add chicken and cook over medium heat 2 to 3 minutes, or until mixture is thoroughly heated. Serve with rice.

8 servings

Chicken à la Winegrower

2 slices bacon, diced
2 cloves garlic, halved
1 tablespoon butter or margarine
4 chicken legs (thighs and drumsticks)
1 cup chopped onion
½ cup dry white wine
2 tablespoons chopped parsley
2 tablespoons chopped chives
1½ teaspoons salt
¼ teaspoon pepper
1 bay leaf
1 can (4 ounces) sliced mushrooms with liquid
1 cup chicken broth
2 tablespoons flour
Hot cooked rice
½ cup dairy sour cream, warmed
Chopped parsley for garnish

1. Sauté bacon and garlic in butter until bacon is partially cooked. Discard garlic.
2. Add chicken and brown on all sides.
3. Stir in onion and sauté until transparent. Add ¼ cup wine and cook a few minutes, stirring to loosen browned particles.
4. Add parsley, chives, seasonings, mushrooms, and broth. Cover and cook over low heat for 30 minutes, or until chicken is tender. Remove chicken and keep warm. Discard bay leaf.
5. Blend flour with remaining wine. Stir into sauce and cook until thickened.
6. Serve chicken on beds of fluffy rice. Top with sauce and dollops of sour cream. Garnish with parsley.

4 servings

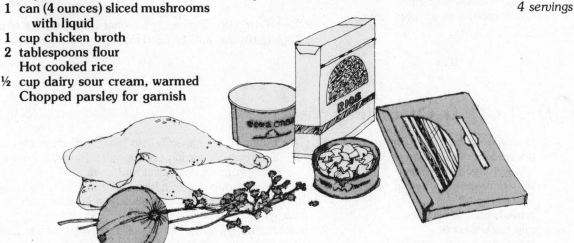

Shrimp Salad with Coral Dressing

Skillet Chicken and Vegetables

1 can (about 10 ounces)
   condensed chicken broth
1 cup dry white wine, such as
   chablis
1 tablespoon instant minced onion
½ teaspoon salt
1 bay leaf
¼ teaspoon rosemary, crushed
6 half breasts of chicken
6 small carrots
6 small zucchini
2 tablespoons cornstarch
2 tablespoons cold water
3 tablespoons chopped pimento
2 tablespoons chopped parsley

1. Combine broth, wine, onion, salt, bay leaf, and rosemary in a large skillet. Heat to boiling.
2. Place chicken breasts in the boiling liquid; cover and simmer 20 minutes.
3. While chicken is cooking, pare carrots and cut in half lengthwise. Cut zucchini in half lengthwise. Add carrots and zucchini to the chicken; cover, and cook 15 minutes longer, or until chicken is tender and vegetables are crisp-tender.
4. Remove chicken and vegetables with a slotted spoon; keep warm.
5. Mix cornstarch with water and stir into liquid remaining in skillet. Cook, stirring until sauce boils thoroughly. Add pimento and parsley, and pour over chicken and vegetables.
Serve immediately.

6 servings

Chicken Marengo

1 broiler-fryer chicken (2 to 3
   pounds)
⅓ cup all-purpose flour
1 teaspoon salt
¼ teaspoon pepper
¼ cup olive oil
1 clove garlic, crushed
3 tablespoons chopped onion
4 tomatoes, quartered
1 cup white wine
   Herb Bouquet
1 cup (about 4 ounces) sliced
   mushrooms
2 tablespoons butter
½ cup sliced olives
½ cup chicken bouillon
2 tablespoons all-purpose flour

1. Disjoint chicken and cut into serving-size pieces. Rinse and pat dry with absorbent paper.
2. Coat chicken evenly with a mixture of flour, salt, and pepper.
3. Heat oil in a large skillet and brown chicken.
4. Add garlic, onion, tomatoes, wine, and Herb Bouquet to chicken; cover and simmer over low heat about ½ hour, or until thickest pieces of chicken are tender when pierced with a fork.
5. Sauté mushrooms in butter and add to chicken with olives.
6. Put bouillon and flour into screw-top jar; cover and shake well.
7. Remove chicken from skillet and discard Herb Bouquet. Gradually add bouillon-flour liquid to mixture in skillet, stirring constantly. Boil 3 to 5 minutes until mixture thickens.
8. Return chicken to sauce; cover and simmer 10 minutes. Arrange chicken on a hot platter. Cover with the sauce.

4 or 5 servings

Herb Bouquet: Tie neatly together **3 or 4 sprigs of parsley, 1 sprig thyme,** and **½ bay leaf.**

Chicken a Seville

3 tablespoons butter or margarine
½ pound fresh mushrooms, cleaned
   and halved lengthwise
3 to 4 tablespoons olive or other
   cooking oil
3 pounds chicken pieces
1 cup uncooked rice
1 large clove garlic, minced
2 cups chicken broth or bouillon

1. Heat butter in a large skillet and stir in mushrooms. Cook until lightly browned, stirring occasionally. Remove from skillet and set aside. Pour oil into skillet and heat.
2. Coat chicken pieces with a blend of **flour, salt,** and **pepper.** Fry in hot oil until browned on all sides. Remove chicken and keep warm.
3. Mix rice and garlic with oil in skillet, then stir in 1 cup of the chicken broth. Turn contents of skillet into a shallow baking dish. Put onions, browned chicken, mushrooms, and olives into dish.

12 very small white onions
1 cup small pimento-stuffed olives
1 cup dry white wine
¾ teaspoon oregano
½ cup toasted blanched almonds, sliced

Pour remaining broth and the wine over all. Sprinkle oregano over chicken.

4. Cook, covered, in a 375°F oven about 45 minutes, or until rice is tender. Remove from oven and top with the nuts.

About 6 servings

Breast of Chicken Savannah

4 large chicken breasts, split
2½ ounces (about ¼ cup) peanut butter
8 thin slices cooked ham
¼ cup sherry
Parmesan Sauce:
¼ cup flour
2 cups milk
½ teaspoon salt
6 tablespoons freshly grated Parmesan cheese
2 tablespoons firm butter

1. Lift skin on chicken breasts slightly, and spread a film of peanut butter on meat under skin; replace skin.
2. Place 1 slice of cooked ham over skin side of each breast.
3. Put sherry into a large casserole or braising pan. Add chicken pieces, ham side up; cover and cook in a 350°F oven 1 hour, or until pieces are tender.
4. Remove breasts from pan and keep warm while preparing Parmesan sauce; reserve ¼ cup pan drippings.
5. For sauce, put the pan drippings into a medium saucepan. Add flour; stir and heat until bubbly. Add milk gradually, stirring well; bring to boiling and cook 1 to 2 minutes.
6. Add salt and Parmesan cheese, stirring until cheese melts. Stir in butter, 1 tablespoon at a time.
7. Pour sauce over chicken and serve.

8 servings

Chicken Mexicana

2 broiler-fryer chickens (2½ to 3 pounds each), cut in serving-size pieces, browned, and partially cooked
2 cans (8 ounces each) tomato sauce
1 can (13¾ ounces) chicken broth
2 tablespoons (½ envelope) dry onion soup mix
¾ cup chopped onion
1 clove garlic, minced
6 tablespoons peanut butter, chunk-style or crunchy
½ cup cream
½ teaspoon chili powder
¼ cup dry sherry
Hot cooked rice

1. While chicken is browning in a large skillet, combine in a saucepan the tomato sauce, 1 cup of the chicken broth, the soup mix, onion, and garlic. Heat thoroughly, stirring constantly. Pour over chicken in skillet. Simmer, covered, 20 minutes.
2. Adding gradually, blend the cream and remaining chicken broth into the peanut butter. Stir into skillet with chili powder and wine. Heat thoroughly. Serve with cooked rice.

6 servings

Chicken, Cacciatore Style

¼ cup vegetable oil
1 broiler-fryer chicken (about 2½ pounds), cut in serving-size pieces
2 medium onions, sliced
2 cloves garlic, crushed in a garlic press or minced
3 tomatoes, sliced
2 medium green peppers, sliced
1 small bay leaf
1 teaspoon salt
¼ teaspoon ground black pepper
½ teaspoon celery seed
1 teaspoon crushed oregano or basil
1 can (8 ounces) tomato sauce
¼ cup dry white wine
8 ounces spaghetti, cooked

1. Heat oil in a large heavy skillet. Add chicken and brown on all sides. Remove chicken from skillet.
2. Add onion and garlic to oil remaining in skillet and cook until onion is tender but not brown; stir occasionally to cook evenly.
3. Return chicken to skillet and add the tomato, green pepper, and bay leaf.
4. Mix salt, pepper, celery seed, and oregano with tomato sauce; pour over all.
5. Cover and cook over low heat 45 minutes. Blend in wine and cook, uncovered, 20 minutes. Discard bay leaf.
6. Put cooked spaghetti onto a warm serving platter and top with the chicken pieces and sauce.

About 6 servings

Herb-Chicken with Mushrooms

2 tablespoons butter or margarine
1 broiler-fryer chicken (3 pounds), cut in quarters
¾ cup cider vinegar
¼ cup water
1 cup (about 3 ounces) sliced mushrooms
1 tablespoon finely chopped parsley
1 tablespoon finely chopped chives
1 teaspoon crushed tarragon
½ teaspoon thyme
½ teaspoon salt
¼ teaspoon black pepper
2 tablespoons flour
1½ cups chicken broth
½ cup sherry

1. Heat butter in a large skillet. Place chicken pieces, skin side down, in skillet and brown on all sides.
2. Meanwhile, pour a mixture of vinegar and water over the mushrooms. Let stand 10 minutes; drain.
3. When chicken is evenly browned, transfer pieces to a shallow baking dish. Sprinkle the seasonings over the chicken. Spoon drained mushrooms over the top; sprinkle evenly with flour. Pour broth and wine over all.
4. Bake at 325°F about 1 hour, or until tender.

About 4 servings

Roast Duckling with Olives

1 duckling (about 4 pounds)
⅓ cup olive oil or other cooking oil
2 medium carrots, coarsely chopped
1 large onion, coarsely chopped
½ teaspoon salt
⅛ teaspoon seasoned pepper
¼ teaspoon rosemary
⅛ teaspoon savory
2 small stalks celery, chopped
3 sprigs parsley, chopped
1 small bay leaf
⅓ cup cognac
2 tablespoons tomato paste
2 cups hot chicken broth or bouillon
⅓ cup dry white wine
16 whole pitted green olives

1. Rinse, pat dry, and cut duckling into quarters. Remove any excess fat from pieces.
2. Heat oil in skillet; add duckling pieces and cook over medium heat until well browned on all sides. Remove pieces from skillet and keep warm.
3. Add carrots, onion, salt, seasoned pepper, rosemary, savory, celery, parsley, and bay leaf to skillet; continue cooking until carrots and onions are lightly browned. Drain off excess fat in skillet.
4. Return duck to skillet and pour cognac over it. Ignite and when flame ceases add a blend of tomato paste, chicken broth, and white wine. Cover skillet and cook in a 350°F oven about 1½ hours, or until duckling is tender.
5. Remove to heated serving platter and keep warm. Strain remaining mixture in skillet into a saucepan and add green olives. Heat until sauce is very hot and pour over duckling.

4 servings

Roast Rock Cornish Hen with Wild Rice and Mushrooms

1½ cups water
½ teaspoon salt
½ cup wild rice
2 tablespoons butter or margarine
½ pound mushrooms, sliced lengthwise through caps and stems
1 tablespoon finely chopped onion
3 tablespoons melted butter or margarine
2 tablespoons madeira
4 Rock Cornish hens, about 1 pound each
2 teaspoons salt
¼ cup unsalted butter, melted
Watercress (optional)

1. Bring the water and salt to boiling in a deep saucepan.
2. Wash rice in a sieve. Add rice gradually to water so that boiling will not stop. Boil rapidly, covered, 30 to 40 minutes, or until a kernel of rice is entirely tender when pressed between fingers. Drain rice in a colander or sieve.
3. While rice is cooking, heat 2 tablespoons butter or margarine in a skillet. Add the mushrooms and onion; cook, stirring occasionally, until mushrooms are lightly browned. Combine mushrooms, wild rice, melted butter, and madeira; toss gently until mushrooms and butter are evenly distributed throughout rice.
4. Rinse and pat hens dry with absorbent paper. Rub cavities of the hens with the salt. Lightly fill body cavities with the wild rice stuffing. To close body cavities, sew or skewer and lace with cord. Fasten neck skin to backs and wings to bodies with skewers.
5. Place hens, breast-side up, on rack in roasting pan. Brush each hen with melted unsalted butter (about 1 tablespoon).
6. Roast, uncovered, in a 350°F oven; frequently baste hens during roasting period with drippings from roasting pan. Roast 1 to 1½ hours, or until hens test done. To test, move leg gently by grasping end bone; drumstick-thigh joint moves easily when hens are done. Remove skewers, if used.
7. Transfer hens to a heated serving platter and garnish with sprigs of watercress if desired.

4 to 8 servings

Roast Goose with Sauerkraut Stuffing

1 goose (ready-to-cook 10 to
    12 pounds)
1 tablespoon butter or margarine
2 large onions, chopped
6½ cups drained sauerkraut, snipped
2 medium apples, quartered,
    cored, and diced
1 small carrot, pared and shredded
2 medium potatoes, shredded
    (about 1½ cups)
½ cup dry white wine
1 to 2 tablespoons brown sugar
2 teaspoons caraway seed
½ teaspoon seasoned pepper
    Salt

1. Singe and clean goose removing any large layers of fat from the body and neck cavities. Rinse thoroughly, drain, and pat dry with absorbent paper; set aside.
2. Heat butter in a skillet; add onion and cook until crisp-tender, 3 to 5 minutes.
3. Meanwhile, combine kraut, apple, carrot, and potato in a large bowl; toss until mixed. Add the onion, wine, and a blend of brown sugar, caraway seed, and seasoned pepper; toss again.
4. Rub cavities of goose with salt; lightly spoon stuffing into the body and neck cavities. Truss goose; set, breast side up, on a rack in a shallow roasting pan.
5. Roast, uncovered, in a 325°F oven about 3½ hours, or until goose tests done. Remove stuffing to a serving dish and accompany with slices of the roast goose.

About 8 servings

Glazed Duckling Gourmet

2 ducklings (about 4 pounds
    each), quartered (do not use
    wings, necks, and backs) and
    skinned
1½ teaspoons salt
¼ teaspoon ground nutmeg
3 to 4 tablespoons butter
1 clove garlic, minced
1½ teaspoons rosemary, crushed
1½ teaspoons thyme
1½ cups burgundy
2 teaspoons red wine vinegar
⅓ cup currant jelly
2 teaspoons cornstarch
2 tablespoons cold water
1½ cups halved seedless green
    grapes
    Watercress

1. Remove excess fat from duckling pieces; rinse duckling and pat dry with absorbent paper. Rub pieces with salt and nutmeg.
2. Heat butter and garlic in a large skillet over medium heat; add the duckling pieces and brown well on all sides.
3. Add rosemary, thyme, burgundy, vinegar, and jelly to skillet. Bring to boiling; cover and simmer over low heat until duckling is tender (about 45 minutes). Remove duckling to a heated platter and keep it warm.
4. Combine cornstarch and water; blend into liquid in skillet; bring to boiling and cook 1 to 2 minutes, stirring constantly. Add grapes and toss them lightly until thoroughly heated.
5. Pour the hot sauce over duckling; garnish platter with watercress.

6 to 8 servings

EGGS, CHEESE, RICE, AND PASTA

Eggs Poached in Wine

1 tablespoon butter or margarine, melted
½ cup dry white wine
4 eggs (yolks whole)
Salt
Seasoned pepper
2 tablespoons Roquefort cheese (crumbled)

1. In a skillet combine butter and wine. When quite hot carefully slip eggs in, one at a time.
2. Season to taste with salt and seasoned pepper. Cook gently until whites of eggs are almost "set." Sprinkle eggs with cheese.
3. Cook several minutes longer, or until cheese is melted. Serve eggs on **buttered toast rounds.**

4 servings

Swiss Cheese Fondue

1 loaf (1 pound) French bread
1 tablespoon cornstarch
2 tablespoons kirsch
1 clove garlic, halved
2 cups dry white wine, such as Neuchâtel
1 pound natural Swiss cheese, shredded
Freshly ground black pepper to taste
Ground nutmeg to taste

1. Cut bread into bite-size pieces each having at least one crusty side; set aside.
2. Mix cornstarch and kirsch in a small bowl; set aside.
3. Rub the inside of a 2-quart flame-resistant casserole or porcelain-finished saucepan with cut surface of garlic. Pour in wine; place over medium heat until wine is about to simmer (do not boil).
4. Add the shredded cheese in small amount to the hot wine, stirring constantly until cheese is melted. Heat cheese-wine mixture until bubbly.
5. Blend in the cornstarch mixture and continue stirring while cooking 5 minutes, or until fondue begins to bubble; add seasoning.
6. Spear bread with forks to use for dipping. Keep the fondue gently bubbling throughout serving time.

About 10 servings

Ham di Parma

8 ounces spaghetti, cooked and drained
¾ cup shredded Parmesan cheese
6 ounces mushrooms, sliced lengthwise
2 tablespoons grated onion
⅓ cup butter or margarine
¼ cup flour
2 cups cream
¾ cup dry white wine
1 pound cooked ham, cut in strips
⅓ cup sliced green olives
1 pimento, cut in thin strips
¼ teaspoon oregano, crushed
⅛ teaspoon black pepper

1. Toss spaghetti with ½ cup cheese; keep hot.
2. Cook mushrooms and onion 5 minutes in hot butter in a large skillet. With a slotted spoon, remove mushrooms; set aside.
3. Blend flour into butter in skillet. Remove from heat and gradually add cream, stirring constantly. Bring to boiling; cook 1 minute. Blend in wine, ham strips, olives, pimento, oregano, and pepper.
4. Put hot spaghetti into a large shallow baking dish. Spoon hot creamed ham mixture over spaghetti. Sprinkle with remaining Parmesan cheese.
5. Broil 4 to 6 inches from heat until lightly browned and thoroughly heated.

About 8 servings

Rice Milanese

¼ cup butter or margarine
¼ cup finely chopped onion
1 cup uncooked rice
3 cups chicken broth
½ cup Marsala
1 teaspoon salt
¼ teaspoon saffron
2 tablespoons hot water
¼ cup grated Parmesan cheese

1. In a heavy 1½-quart saucepan with a tight-fitting cover, melt butter. Add and cook onion until lightly browned. Stir in uncooked rice. Cook slowly until rice is lightly browned, stirring with a fork.
2. Add broth, wine, and salt slowly, stirring with a fork until mixture boils. Cover pan, reduce heat, and allow rice to simmer without stirring 18 minutes. Turn off heat and leave pan in place; do not lift cover as rice must steam.
3. Meanwhile, dissolve saffron in hot water.
4. Water in saucepan should be absorbed in 30 minutes and rice tender, fluffy, and dry. Add saffron mixture to rice. Mix well using a fork to lift and turn rice.
5. Serve warm, topped with cheese.

3 to 4 cups rice

Saffron Rice

3 cups well-seasoned chicken broth
1 cup dry white wine
1 teaspoon chopped scallions
1 teaspoon chopped parsley
½ teaspoon powdered saffron
½ teaspoon coriander
½ teaspoon fennel
⅛ teaspoon mace
2 cups uncooked long grain rice
2 to 3 tablespoons butter

1. In a large saucepan, combine chicken broth, wine, scallions, parsley, saffron, coriander, fennel, and mace. Bring rapidly to boiling over high heat.
2. Add the rice all at once; do not stir. Cover tightly so that no steam escapes. Turn the heat as low as possible. Cook for 30 minutes.
3. Stir in butter and serve.

About 8 servings

SALADS

Shrimp Salad with Coral Dressing

2 cups cooked, peeled, and deveined shrimp
1½ cups cooked rice
½ cup sliced celery
½ cup chopped unpeeled cucumbers
¼ cup chopped chives
⅓ cup mayonnaise
¼ cup dairy sour cream
1 tablespoon chili sauce
¼ teaspoon onion salt
⅛ teaspoon pepper
1½ teaspoons tarragon vinegar
Salad greens
Horseradish (optional)
Lemon wedges

1. Toss shrimp, rice, celery, cucumbers, and chives together.
2. Blend ingredients for dressing. Pour over shrimp mixture and toss thoroughly. Chill.
3. Serve on salad greens. Top with a little horseradish, if desired, and garnish with lemon wedges.
4. Accompany with champagne.

6 servings

Gourmet Salad Dressing

3 ounces Roquefort cheese,
　　crumbled (about ¾ cup)
1 package (3 ounces) cream
　　cheese, softened
1 cup dairy sour cream
⅓ cup sherry
1 tablespoon grated onion
½ teaspoon salt
¼ teaspoon paprika
1 or 2 drops Tabasco

1. Put Roquefort cheese into a bowl. Blend in cream cheese until smooth.
2. Add sour cream, sherry, onion, salt, paprika, and Tabasco; blend until creamy. Store dressing, covered, in refrigerator.

About 2 cups dressing

Enchanting Fruit Dressing

A fitting partner for fruit.

½ cup water
½ cup honey
8 mint leaves
⅛ teaspoon whole cardamom
　　seed (contents of 3
　　cardamom pods), crushed
¼ teaspoon salt
½ cup sherry, madeira, or port
1 tablespoon lemon juice

1. Put water, honey, mint leaves (bruise the mint with the back of a spoon), and cardamom seed into a small saucepan with a tight-fitting cover. Set over low heat and stir until mixed. Cover saucepan and bring rapidly to boiling. Boil gently 5 minutes. Remove from heat and stir in salt. Set aside to cool.
2. When mixture is cool, strain it and blend in sherry and lemon juice.

About 1⅓ cups dressing

Speedy Seafood Aspic

2 envelopes unflavored gelatin
1 can (12 ounces) cocktail
　　vegetable juice
1 can (12 ounces) pineapple juice
1 tablespoon chopped chives
½ teaspoon seasoned salt
¼ teaspoon thyme
½ cup dry white wine
2 cans (4½ ounces each) shrimp,
　　drained
Crisp salad greens

1. Soften gelatin in cocktail vegetable juice in saucepan. Heat to boiling, stirring constantly to dissolve. Remove from heat.
2. Blend in pineapple juice, chives, seasoned salt, and thyme. Stir in wine. Chill until mixture thickens to consistency of unbeaten egg white.
3. Fold in drained shrimp. Turn into a 1-quart mold. Chill until firm.
4. Unmold onto crisp salad greens.

4 to 6 servings

Salde Siciliano

1 whole clove garlic
4 anchovy fillets
  Juice of 1 lemon
6 tablespoons dry red wine, such as burgundy
¾ cup olive oil
  Oregano leaves (¼ ounce or 2½ tablespoons)
  Peppercorns, crushed (⅛ ounce or ¾ teaspoon)
2 cloves garlic, minced
1 pimento, diced
3 tomatoes, diced
1 cup cooked green beans
1 cup diced hearts of artichoke
1 cup diced hearts of palm
1 head romaine lettuce, torn in pieces
1 head iceberg lettuce, torn in chunks
2 slices bread, toasted and cut in cubes
¼ pound Gorgonzola cheese, crumbled

1. Rub a large wooden salad bowl with the whole clove of garlic. Add anchovy fillets. Rub bowl again with the garlic and anchovies; mash together forming a paste. Blend in, stirring vigorously, the lemon juice, burgundy, olive oil, oregano, and pepper. (If necessary, correct seasonings to taste.)
2. Blend in minced garlic, diced pimento, and tomatoes. Add green beans, hearts of artichoke and palm, romaine, and iceberg lettuce. Toss lightly.
3. Add croutons and cheese. Again, toss lightly. Serve immediately on chilled salad plates.

4 to 8 servings

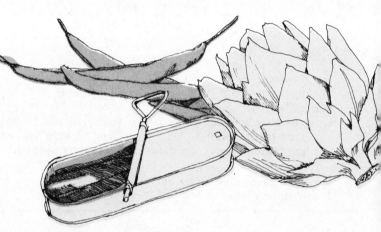

White Wine Aspic

1½ tablespoons unflavored gelatin
2 tablespoons sugar
¼ teaspoon salt
⅔ cup cold water
1¼ cups apple juice
1 cup dry white wine, such as chablis
1 tablespoon sweet pickle syrup
1 tablespoon lemon juice
½ cup dairy sour cream

1. Blend gelatin, sugar, and salt in a saucepan; add water. Place over low heat, stirring constantly, until gelatin and sugar are thoroughly dissolved.
2. Stir in apple juice, white wine, pickle syrup, and lemon juice. Chill until slightly thickened. Immediately blend with sour cream.
3. Pour into a fancy 1-quart ring mold and chill until firm. Unmold onto a serving plate and surround with fresh fruits, such as peach or pear halves or wedges, bunches of Tokay or green grapes, sweet red cherries, orange segments, or other colorful fruits in season.

About 6 servings

Note: If desired, fold 1½ cups shredded vegetables such as carrots, cabbage, cucumber, and green pepper into sour cream-gelatin mixture and turn into an 8×8×2-inch pan. Chill until firm, cut into squares, and serve in crisp lettuce cups.

Chicken Mousse Amandine

½ cup dry white wine, such as sauterne
2 envelopes unflavored gelatin
3 egg yolks
1 cup milk
1 cup chicken broth

1. Place a small bowl and a rotary beater in refrigerator to chill.
2. Pour wine into a small cup and sprinkle gelatin evenly over wine; set aside.
3. Beat egg yolks slightly in top of a double boiler; add milk gradually, stirring constantly.
4. Stir in the chicken broth gradually. Cook over simmering

½ cup (about 3 ounces) almonds, finely chopped
3 cups ground cooked chicken
¼ cup mayonnaise
2 tablespoons minced parsley
2 tablespoons chopped green olives
1 teaspoon lemon juice
1 teaspoon onion juice
½ teaspoon salt
½ teaspoon celery salt
Few grains paprika
Few grains cayenne pepper
½ cup chilled heavy cream
Sprigs of parsley

water, stirring constantly and rapidly until mixture coats a metal spoon.

5. Remove from heat. Stir softened gelatin and immediately stir it into the hot mixture until gelatin is completely dissolved. Cool; chill in refrigerator or over ice and water until gelatin mixture begins to gel (becomes slightly thicker). If mixture is placed over ice and water, stir frequently; if placed in refrigerator, stir occasionally.

6. Blend almonds and chicken into chilled custard mixture along with mayonnaise, parsley, olives, lemon juice, onion juice, and a mixture of salt, celery salt, paprika, and cayenne pepper.

7. Using the chilled bowl and beater, beat cream until of medium consistency (piles softly).

8. Fold whipped cream into chicken mixture. Turn into a 1½-quart fancy mold. Chill in refrigerator until firm.

9. Unmold onto chilled serving plate and, if desired, garnish with sprigs of parsley.

8 servings

Dubonnet Chicken Salad Mold

2 envelopes unflavored gelatin
1 cup cranberry juice cocktail
1 cup red Dubonnet
1 cup red currant syrup
1 envelope unflavored gelatin
¾ cup cold water
1 tablespoon soy sauce
1 cup mayonnaise
1½ cups finely diced cooked chicken
½ cup finely chopped celery
¼ cup toasted blanched almonds, finely chopped
½ cup whipping cream, whipped
Leaf lettuce
Cucumber slices, scored
Pitted ripe olives

1. Soften 2 envelopes gelatin in cranberry juice in a saucepan; set over low heat and stir until gelatin is dissolved. Remove from heat and stir in Dubonnet and currant syrup.

2. Pour into a 2-quart fancy tube mold. Chill until set but not firm.

3. Meanwhile, soften 1 envelope gelatin in cold water in a saucepan. Set over low heat and stir until gelatin is dissolved.

4. Remove from heat and stir in soy sauce and mayonnaise until thoroughly blended. Chill until mixture becomes slightly thicker. Mix in chicken, celery, and almonds. Fold in whipped cream until blended.

5. Spoon mixture into mold over first layer. Chill 8 hours or overnight.

6. Unmold onto a chilled serving plate. Garnish with lettuce, cucumber, and olives.

About 10 servings

Peach Wine Mold

1 can (29 ounces) sliced peaches
1 package (6 ounces) lemon-flavored gelatin
1½ cups boiling water
1 cup white wine
⅓ cup sliced celery
⅓ cup slivered blanched almonds
Curly endive

1. Drain peaches thoroughly, reserving 1¼ cups syrup. Reserve and refrigerate about 8 peach slices for garnish. Cut remaining peaches into pieces; set aside.

2. Pour gelatin into a bowl, add boiling water, and stir until gelatin is dissolved. Stir in reserved syrup and wine. Chill until partially set.

3. Mix peaches, celery, and almonds into gelatin. Turn into a 1½-quart fancy mold. Chill until firm.

4. Unmold salad onto a serving plate. Garnish with curly endive and reserved peach slices.

About 8 servings

Golden Glow Salad

1 **package (6 ounces) lemon-flavored gelatin**
2 **cups boiling water**
1 **can (20 ounces) crushed pineapple**
1 **cup dry white wine, such as chablis**
2 **cups grated carrots**
  Crisp salad greens

1. Dissolve gelatin in boiling water.
2. Drain pineapple, reserving 1 cup syrup.
3. Add pineapple syrup and wine to gelatin mixture. Chill until partially set.
4. Fold in carrots and pineapple. Fill 12 individual molds or one 1½-quart mold.
5. Chill until firm and unmold on greens.

12 servings

VEGETABLES

Sauerkraut Casserole

1 **tablespoon butter or margarine**
2 **large onions, chopped**
6½ **cups drained sauerkraut, snipped**
2 **medium apples, quartered, cored, and diced**
1 **small carrot, pared and shredded**
2 **medium potatoes, shredded (about 1½ cups)**
½ **cup dry white wine**
1 **to 2 tablespoons brown sugar**
2 **teaspoons caraway seed**
½ **teaspoon seasoned pepper**
  Brown sugar
  Apple, thinly sliced

1. Heat butter in a skillet. Add onion and cook, stirring occasionally, until crisp-tender, 3 to 5 minutes.
2. Meanwhile, combine kraut, diced apple, carrot, and potato in a large bowl. Toss until mixed.
3. Add onion, wine, 1 to 2 tablespoons brown sugar, caraway seed, and seasoned pepper. Toss again. Turn into a 2-quart casserole; sprinkle generously with brown sugar.
4. Overlap thinly sliced apple on top; sprinkle again with brown sugar.
5. Heat in a 350°F oven until thoroughly heated and apples are tender.

10 to 12 servings

Beets in Red Wine Sauce

2 tablespoons butter
1 shallot, minced
2 tablespoons flour
1 jar or can (16 ounces) beets, drained and ⅓ cup liquid reserved
⅓ cup beef bouillon
⅓ cup red wine
Ground cloves (optional)

1. Melt butter in a saucepan; stir in minced shallot. Add flour, stirring constantly for 1 minute.
2. Blend reserved beef liquid, bouillon, and red wine into flour mixture; bring to boiling, stirring until sauce is smooth and thick. Sprinkle lightly with cloves, if desired.
3. Add beets and heat thoroughly.

4 to 6 servings

Red Cabbage and Wine

1 head (about 2 pounds) red cabbage
1 cup red wine
⅓ cup firmly packed brown sugar
1 teaspoon salt
Few grains cayenne pepper
4 medium apples
¼ cup cider vinegar
¼ cup butter

1. Remove and discard wilted outer leaves of cabbage. Rinse, cut into quarters (discarding core), and coarsely shred (about 2 quarts, shredded). Put cabbage into a saucepan with wine, brown sugar, salt, and pepper.
2. Rinse, quarter, core, and pare apples. Add the apples to the saucepan.
3. Cover and simmer over low heat 20 to 30 minutes, or until cabbage is tender. Add vinegar and butter. Toss together lightly until butter is melted.

6 servings

Celery Coronado

3 celery hearts
1 tablespoon green pepper, chopped
¼ cup butter or margarine
1 cup chicken bouillon or broth
½ cup dry white wine, such as sauterne
1 small jar pimentos
Sliced almonds, sautéed

1. Wash celery and split lengthwise. Sauté celery and green pepper in butter, turning celery gently.
2. Add bouillon and wine. Cover and cook over low heat until celery is tender-crisp.
3. Remove celery to heat-resistant platter and keep warm in oven.
4. Reduce the sauce until it has a glazed appearance. Pour it over the celery. Garnish with strips of pimento and sautéed almonds.

4 to 6 servings

Mushrooms in Wine Sauce on Toast

1 cup water
½ cup white wine
3 tablespoons butter
1 pound fresh mushrooms, cleaned
1 tablespoon flour
Juice of ½ lemon
1 egg yolk
¼ cup light cream
4 slices toast, sliced diagonally

1. Combine water, wine, and 1 tablespoon of the butter; add to the mushrooms in a saucepan. Bring to boiling; cover and let simmer 10 minutes. Drain, reserving broth.
2. Heat 2 tablespoons butter and blend in flour. Gradually add reserved broth, stirring constantly. Bring to boiling; stir and cook 1 to 2 minutes.
3. Thinly slice the mushrooms; mix into sauce with lemon juice. Cook 5 minutes.
4. Beat the egg yolk with cream. Gradually add mushroom mixture and mix well. Serve mushrooms on toast points.

4 servings

Sweet and Sour Red Cabbage

1 head (2 pounds) red cabbage
4 tablespoons brown sugar
1 teaspoon salt
½ cup beef bouillon
¼ cup cider vinegar
4 slices bacon, diced
4 tablespoons butter
2 medium cooking (sour) apples, pared and sliced
1 cup red wine

1. Discard tough, outer leaves of cabbage and shred, as for cole slaw.
2. Combine brown sugar, salt, bouillon, and vinegar as a marinade. Let cabbage stand in marinade 1 hour or longer. (This cabbage is limp when served so can be marinated as long as you wish.)
3. Cook bacon until crisp; drain bacon pieces, and pour off all but 2 tablespoons of bacon fat.
4. Melt butter in bacon fat. Add cabbage, marinade and all. Arrange apples on top of cabbage. Cover and cook slowly 1 hour.
5. Add wine, cover, and simmer 30 minutes.

6 servings

Macaroni Vegetable Medley au Vin

2 cups (8 ounces) elbow macaroni
1 package (10 ounces) frozen mixed vegetables
2 tablespoons butter or margarine
3 ounces fresh mushrooms, chopped
½ cup chopped onion
1 can (about 10 ounces) condensed cream of celery soup
1 soup can milk
2 teaspoons Worcestershire sauce
1 teaspoon salt
¼ teaspoon white pepper
1 teaspoon dry mustard
½ cup dry sherry or dry white wine
¼ cup chopped pimento
1 cup cooked peas
½ pound Swiss cheese, shredded
Chopped parsley
Pimento strips

1. Cook macaroni and frozen vegetables following directions on package. Drain and set aside.
2. Heat butter in a skillet; add mushrooms and onion. Cook, stirring occasionally, until onion is soft; set aside.
3. In a large bowl mix soup, milk, Worcestershire sauce, salt, white pepper, dry mustard, and wine. Add chopped pimento, peas, cheese, mushroom mixture, mixed vegetables, and macaroni; mix well. Turn into a greased 2½-quart casserole.
4. Bake at 300°F until thoroughly heated, about 30 minutes. Garnish with chopped parsley and pimento strips.

About 8 servings

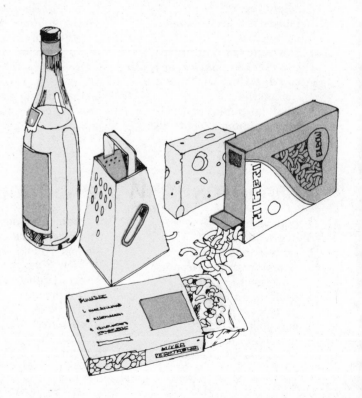

Celery and Green Pepper au Gratin

4 cups diagonally sliced celery
2 green peppers, thinly sliced
¼ cup dry sherry
3 tablespoons butter or
    margarine, melted
1 cup soft bread crumbs
½ cup crumbled blue cheese

1. Cook celery and green pepper, covered, in a small amount of boiling salted water until crisp-tender (about 5 minutes); drain. Turn vegetables into a shallow 1½-quart baking dish and drizzle with 3 tablespoons sherry.
2. Mix remaining sherry with butter and toss with bread crumbs and blue cheese. Spoon over vegetables.
3. Set under broiler with top 3 to 4 inches from heat. Broil until top is lightly browned.

6 to 8 servings

SAUCES

Brown or Espagnole Sauce

Serve with meat, chicken, and some vegetables, such as green beans and eggplant.

¼ cup chopped green onion
½ cup chopped celery
½ cup chopped carrot
2 tablespoons cooking oil
2 quarts water
3 beef bouillon cubes
3 chicken bouillon cubes
1 small bay leaf
   Pinch ground thyme
   Few grains freshly ground
      black pepper
2 tablespoons tomato sauce
½ cup water
¼ cup flour

1. Using a large saucepot, cook onion, celery, and carrot in hot oil until dark brown; do not burn. Add 2 quarts water, bouillon cubes, bay leaf, thyme, and pepper; bring to boiling and then simmer until stock is reduced by half.
2. Strain. Stir in tomato sauce; bring to boiling.
3. Vigorously shake the ½ cup water and flour in a screw-top jar. Gradually add to boiling mixture, stirring constantly. Cook 1 to 2 minutes, then simmer about 30 minutes, stirring occasionally.

1 quart sauce

Sauce Piquante

Serve with variety meats, such as liver and kidneys, and with leftover roast meats.

¼ cup dry white wine
1 tablespoon vinegar
1 tablespoon butter
2 teaspoons minced shallot
1 cup Brown Sauce (this page)
1 tablespoon finely minced
   parsley
1 tablespoon tart pickle relish
   or 2 tablespoons minced sour
   gherkins

Combine wine, vinegar, butter, and shallot. Boil until liquid is reduced by half. Stir in brown sauce, parsley, and pickle relish. Serve hot.

1 cup sauce

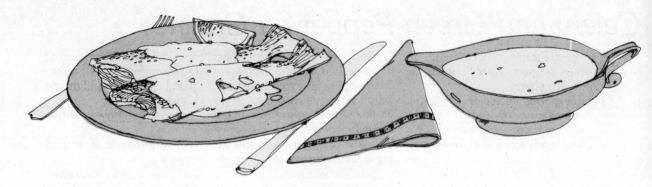

Sauce Velouté (Velvet Sauce)

Serve with fish, croquettes, or eggs.

3 tablespoons butter
3 tablespoons flour
¼ teaspoon salt
⅛ teaspoon white pepper
1½ cups fish stock
½ teaspoon nutmeg

1. Melt butter in a saucepan over low heat. Stir in until well blended a mixture of flour, salt, and white pepper.
2. Heat until mixture bubbles. Remove from heat and gradually stir in ½ cup of the fish stock.
3. Return to heat and bring rapidly to boiling, stirring constantly. Cook 1 to 2 minutes longer; gradually blend in remaining fish stock.
4. Boil 1 to 2 minutes, stirring constantly, until thick and smooth. Stir in nutmeg.

About 1½ cups sauce

Sauce Robert

Serve with beefsteaks and pork.

¼ cup finely chopped onion
3 tablespoons butter
½ cup dry white wine
2 tablespoons white wine
   vinegar
1 cup Brown Sauce (page 79)
2 tablespoons tomato sauce
   Salt and pepper
1 tablespoon prepared mustard

1. Sauté onion in butter until golden. Add wine and vinegar and reduce by half.
2. Stir in the brown and tomato sauces. Add salt and pepper to taste. Simmer slowly for 10 minutes. At the last moment, blend in the mustard.

About 1½ cups sauce

Bercy Sauce (Wine-Merchant Sauce)

Serve with poached fish.

¼ cup chopped shallots
2 tablespoons butter
1 cup white wine
1 cup fish stock
⅔ cup Sauce Velouté (this page)
½ cup butter
2 tablespoons chopped parsley
1½ tablespoons lemon juice

1. Cook shallots in butter without browning, stirring occasionally.
2. Blend in white wine and fish stock. Simmer until reduced to one third the quantity. Stir in Sauce Velouté; continue slow cooking about 5 minutes, or until sauce is clear. Strain.
3. Just before serving, stir in butter, ½ teaspoon at a time.
4. Blend in parsley and lemon juice. Serve hot.

About 1¾ cups sauce

Glazed Apple Tart in Wheat Germ Crus

Barbecue Sauce with Wine

Basting sauce for meats on the grill.

1 cup dry red wine
½ cup salad or cooking oil
½ cup red wine vinegar
1 tablespoon Worcestershire
   sauce
½ cup finely chopped onion
1 clove garlic, minced
5 tablespoons sugar
½ teaspoon salt
½ teaspoon seasoned pepper
1 tablespoon finely chopped
   parsley
½ teaspoon crushed rosemary
¼ teaspoon crumbled bay leaves
6 whole cloves

Combine all ingredients in a screw-top jar. Cover; shake to blend. Store in the refrigerator. Shake before using.

About 2½ cups sauce

Cheese Sauce for Broccoli

2 tablespoons butter or margarine
2 tablespoons flour
½ teaspoon salt
1 cup milk
¼ cup dry white wine, such as
   sauterne
½ cup grated pasteurized process
   Swiss cheese
Dash each white pepper and
   nutmeg
1 tablespoon chopped pimento
   (optional)

1. Melt butter and blend in flour and salt.
2. Add milk, stirring until smooth; cook and stir until sauce boils and is thickened.
3. Add wine, cheese, pepper, nutmeg, and pimento, if desired. Stir over low heat until cheese is melted.
4. Spoon hot sauce over **cooked broccoli spears.**

About 1½ cups sauce

Wine Sauce for Game or Tongue

1 tablespoon butter or
   margarine
⅓ cup currant jelly
Juice of ½ lemon
Dash cayenne pepper
½ cup water
3 whole cloves
1 teaspoon salt
½ cup port wine

Combine all ingredients except wine in a saucepan; simmer about 5 minutes. Strain and mix in wine.

About 1 cup sauce

Sherried Holiday Pudding

Bordelaise Sauce

Serve with red meats.

4 shallots, finely chopped
2 to 3 tablespoons butter
1 cup red wine
1 cup Brown Sauce (page 79)
Few drops lemon juice
1 teaspoon finely minced parsley

1. Sauté shallots in butter in a small saucepan. Add the wine and cook over low heat until reduced to one half.
2. Strain. Add Brown Sauce and continue heating. Add lemon juice and parsley.

About 1½ cups sauce

Ravigote Sauce (Green Herb Sauce)

Serve with poultry, eggs, variety meats, such as liver, and leftover roast meat.

½ cup white wine
¼ cup tarragon or wine vinegar
1 shallot, minced
2 cups Sauce Velouté (page 80)
2 tablespoons butter
1 teaspoon minced chervil
1 teaspoon minced tarragon
1 teaspoon chopped chives

1. Combine wine, vinegar, and shallot and simmer in a saucepan.
2. When the liquid is reduced to less than one half, add Sauce Velouté. Heat.
3. Just before serving thoroughly blend in butter, chervil, tarragon, and chives.

About 2¼ cups sauce

Chasseur (Hunter's) Sauce

Serve with eggs or game meats.

1 Belgian shallot, finely minced
1 cup sliced fresh mushrooms
¼ cup butter
½ teaspoon salt
Dash of freshly ground pepper
½ cup dry white wine
1 cup Brown Sauce (page 79)
2 tablespoons tomato sauce
2 tablespoons butter
1 tablespoon finely chopped parsley

1. Sauté shallot and mushrooms in ¼ cup butter, adding salt and pepper. When mushrooms are golden brown, stir in the wine and reduce by half.
2. Blend in the brown and tomato sauces. Bring to boiling, then simmer gently for 15 minutes, stirring occasionally.
3. Add 2 tablespoons butter and parsley. Cook 2 minutes longer, stirring until blended.

2 cups sauce

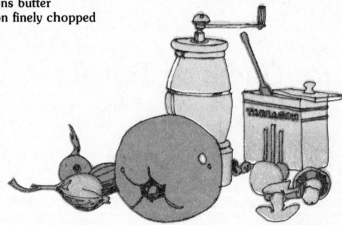

Rich Chocolate Sauce

½ cup butter
2 ounces unsweetened chocolate
    (squares, cut up, or
    envelopes)
½ cup cocoa
¾ cup sugar
1 can (5½ ounces) evaporated
    milk; undiluted
    Few grains of salt
½ cup sherry

1. Combine butter, chocolate, cocoa, sugar, milk, and salt in a saucepan.
2. Cook over low heat, stirring, until the chocolate is melted and mixture is well blended.
3. When the sauce is simmering, not boiling, remove from heat and cool.
4. Add sherry; stir to mix.

About 2 cups sauce

DESSERTS

Wine Fruit Compote

1 can (16 ounces) pear halves
1 can (16 ounces) cling peach
    halves
1 can (13½ ounces) pineapple
    chunks
½ lemon, thinly sliced and
    quartered
2 cups fruit juices and water
5 whole cloves
1 stick cinnamon
1 package (3 ounces) strawberry-
    flavored gelatin
2 teaspoons lemon juice
1 cup cherry kijafa wine

1. Drain fruit and reserve juice. Arrange fruit in a shallow 1½-quart dish. Scatter lemon slices over top.
2. Combine juices from fruit and water, cloves, and cinnamon in a saucepan. Heat to boiling. Simmer for 5 minutes. Strain.
3. Dissolve gelatin in the hot liquid. Add lemon juice and cherry wine. Pour over fruit. Chill 1 to 1½ hours, or until gelatin is only partly set. Baste fruit occasionally with gelatin mixture while chilling.

6 to 8 servings

Elegant Creamed Peaches

1 envelope plain gelatin
½ cup sweet red wine, such as
    port or muscatel
1 pint whipping cream
3 tablespoons powdered sugar
    Dash salt
1 can (29 ounces) cling peach
    halves
½ cup glacé fruit
2 tablespoons roasted diced
    almonds
1 tablespoon honey
1 tablespoon sweet red wine

1. Combine gelatin and ½ cup wine in saucepan; place over low heat and stir until gelatin is dissolved.
2. Cool until mixture begins to thicken.
3. Whip cream with powdered sugar and salt.
4. Fold gelatin mixture into whipped cream. Spoon into 6 to 8 dessert dishes or 9-inch round pan.
5. Drain peaches; place cup-sides up in cream mixture.
6. Combine glacé fruit, almonds, honey, and 1 tablespoon wine. Spoon into peach cups. Chill.

6 to 8 servings

Stuffed Peaches

½ cup almond macaroon crumbs
6 large firm peaches
½ cup blanched almonds, chopped
2 tablespoons sugar
1 tablespoon chopped candied orange peel
⅓ cup sherry or Marsala
2 tablespoons sugar

1. Using an electric blender, grind enough almond macaroons to make ½ cup crumbs. Set crumbs aside.
2. Rinse, peel, and cut peaches into halves. Remove pit and a small portion of the pulp around cavity.
3. Combine and mix macaroon crumbs, chopped almonds, 2 tablespoons sugar, and orange peel.
4. Lightly fill peach halves with mixture. Put two halves together and fasten with wooden picks. Place in baking dish.
5. Pour sherry over peaches and sprinkle remaining sugar over peaches.
6. Bake at 350°F 15 minutes and serve either hot or cold.

6 servings

Port Wine Molds

1 envelope unflavored gelatin
1¼ cups sparkling water
½ cup ruby port
⅓ cup sugar

1. Soften gelatin in ½ cup of the sparkling water. Dissolve over hot water.
2. Combine remaining sparkling water, wine, and sugar; stir until sugar is dissolved. Mix in the gelatin.
3. Pour into 6 individual molds and chill until firm.
4. Unmold gelatin onto a chilled serving plate. Serve as a meat accompaniment.

6 servings

Sherry Elegance

3 envelopes unflavored gelatin
1½ cups sugar
3 cups water
1 cup plus 2 tablespoons sherry
¾ cup strained orange juice
⅓ cup strained lemon juice
9 drops red food coloring

1. Combine the gelatin and sugar in a large saucepan; mix well. Add water and stir over low heat until gelatin and sugar are dissolved.
2. Remove from heat and blend in remaining ingredients. Pour mixture into a 1½-quart fancy mold or a pretty china bowl. Chill until firm.
3. To serve, unmold gelatin onto chilled platter or serve in china bowl without unmolding. Serve with whipped cream or whipped dessert topping, if desired.

6 to 8 servings

Biscuit Tortoni

⅓ cup confectioners' sugar
1 tablespoon sherry
½ cup plus 2 tablespoons fine dry
   macaroon crumbs
1 cup whipping cream, whipped
1 egg white

1. Fold sugar, sherry, and ½ cup macaroon crumbs into whipped cream until well blended.
2. Beat egg white until stiff, not dry, peaks are formed. Fold into whipped cream mixture.
3. Divide mixture equally into ten 2-inch heavy paper baking cups and sprinkle with the remaining crumbs. Freeze until firm.

10 servings

Sherry Almond Chiffon Pie

1 unbaked 9-inch pastry shell
¼ cup blanched almonds, toasted
   (see Note)
⅓ cup sugar
1 envelope unflavored gelatin
½ teaspoon salt
3 egg yolks, slightly beaten
1¾ cups milk
½ cup chilled heavy cream
3 egg whites
¼ cup sugar
3 tablespoons sherry
½ teaspoon almond extract
1 ounce (1 square) unsweetened
   chocolate

1. Chill a bowl and a rotary beater in refrigerator.
2. Bake pastry shell and set aside to cool.
3. Coarsely chop toasted almonds and set aside.
4. Mix ⅓ cup sugar, gelatin, and salt thoroughly in the top of a double boiler.
5. Beat egg yolks with milk until blended; add the milk mixture gradually to gelatin mixture in double boiler top, stirring constantly until blended.
6. Set over boiling water and cook, stirring constantly, until gelatin is completely dissolved, about 5 minutes.
7. Remove the gelatin mixture from heat. Cool; chill in refrigerator or over ice and water until the mixture mounds when dropped from a spoon. (If mixture is placed over ice and water, stir frequently; if placed in refrigerator, stir occasionally.)
8. Beat cream until medium consistency (piles softly) using chilled bowl and beater. Set whipped cream in refrigerator while preparing the meringue.
9. Using a clean beater, beat egg whites until frothy; add ¼ cup sugar gradually, beating well after each addition. Beat until stiff peaks are formed.
10. Fold the meringue and whipped cream into custard mixture with sherry and almond extract. Fold in the chopped toasted almonds. Turn into cooled pie shell.
11. Chill in refrigerator 2 to 3 hours, or until firm. When ready to serve, top with chocolate curls made by pulling chocolate across a shredder.

One 9-inch pie

Note: To toast almonds, place nuts in a shallow baking dish or pie pan and, if desired, brush lightly with butter, margarine, or cooking oil. Heat in a 350°F oven until delicately browned; move and turn occasionally. Or put nuts into a heavy skillet in which butter (about 1 tablespoon per cup of nuts) has been heated. Heat until nuts are lightly browned, moving and turning constantly.

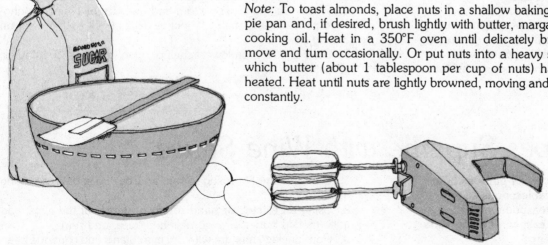

Glazed Apple Tart in Wheat Germ Crust

Wheat Germ Crust (see recipe)
8 medium apples
1 cup red port
1 cup water
⅓ cup honey
2 tablespoons lemon juice
⅛ teaspoon salt
3 drops red food coloring
1 package (8 ounces) cream cheese
1 tablespoon half-and-half
1 tablespoon honey
1½ tablespoons cornstarch

1. Prepare crust and set aside to cool.
2. Pare, core, and cut apples into eighths to make 2 quarts.
3. Combine port, water, ⅓ cup honey, lemon juice, salt, and food coloring in large skillet with a cover. Add half the apples in single layer, cover, and cook slowly about 5 minutes, until apples are barely tender. Remove apples with slotted spoon and arrange in a single layer in a shallow pan. Cook remaining apples in same manner. Chill apples, saving cooking liquid for glaze.
4. Beat cream cheese with half-and-half and 1 tablespoon honey. Spread in even layer over bottom of cooled crust, saving about ¼ cup for decoration on top of tart, if desired.
5. Arrange apples over cheese.
6. Boil syrup from cooking apples down to 1 cup.
7. Mix cornstarch with 1½ tablespoons cold water. Stir into syrup, and cook, stirring, until mixture clears and thickens. Set pan in cold water, and cool quickly to room temperature. Spoon carefully over apples.
8. Chill until glaze is set before cutting.

One 10-inch tart

Wheat Germ Crust

1½ cups sifted all-purpose flour
3 tablespoons wheat germ
3 tablespoons packed brown sugar
¾ teaspoon salt
⅛ teaspoon cinnamon
6 tablespoons shortening
2 tablespoons butter
2 tablespoons milk (about)

1. Combine flour, wheat germ, brown sugar, salt, and cinnamon in mixing bowl.
2. Cut in shortening and butter as for pie crust.
3. Sprinkle with just enough milk to make dough stick together.
4. Press dough against bottom and up sides of 10-inch springform pan to make shell 1¾ inches deep. Prick bottom. Set on baking sheet.
5. Bake at 375°F on lowest shelf of oven for about 20 minutes, or until golden.

Crêpes Superbe with Wine Sauce

⅔ cup all-purpose flour
3 tablespoons sugar
¼ teaspoon salt
⅛ teaspoon baking soda
2 eggs

1. Combine the flour, sugar, salt, and baking soda in a mixing bowl; mix well.
2. Using an electric or hand rotary beater, beat the eggs; add milk, melted butter, orange peel and juice, and rum.
3. Combine egg mixture with dry ingredients and continue beat-

¾ cup milk
¼ cup butter or margarine,
   melted and cooled
1½ teaspoons grated orange peel
3 tablespoons orange juice
1 tablespoon rum

Wine Sauce:
1½ tablespoons butter or
   margarine
1½ teaspoons sugar
¾ cup apricot jam
1 cup port wine
3 tablespoons brandy
3 tablespoons Cointreau or rum

ing until smooth. (Batter should be consistency of heavy cream. Add more orange juice, if necessary.)

4. Heat and lightly butter the bottom of a 6- or 8-inch skillet. Pour in about 2 tablespoons of the batter and tilt skillet to spread batter evenly. Cook over medium heat until small bubbles form in the batter. Turn over and brown crêpe very lightly on second side. Repeat process using all the batter.

5. Keep crêpes warm by placing them in a pan over simmering water.

6. For wine sauce, heat butter in a chafing dish blazer over direct heat. Stir in sugar, jam, port wine, brandy, and Cointreau. Heat until mixture comes to boiling. Reduce heat and ignite the sauce.

7. To serve, roll crêpes jelly-roll fashion on serving plates; allow 2 or 3 per serving. Ladle hot wine sauce over them.

6 to 8 servings

Chocolate Cream Cups

1 package (3 ounces) chocolate
   or butterscotch pudding
1½ cups milk
¼ cups sherry
1 teaspoon instant coffee powder
⅛ teaspoon salt
½ cup whipping cream, whipped

Spiced Cream Topping:
½ cup whipping cream, whipped
1 tablespoon sugar
½ teaspoon instant coffee powder
⅛ teaspoon cinnamon

1. Prepare pudding mix according to package directions using milk and sherry for the liquid.

2. Add instant coffee and salt. Cover and chill.

3. Fold in whipped cream and spoon into 6 or 8 individual serving dishes. Serve with a bowl of Spiced Cream Topping.

4. For Spiced Cream Topping, whip cream; fold in sugar, instant coffee powder, and cinnamon.

6 to 8 servings

Trifle

Day-old pound cake (enough
   to line bottom of casserole)
½ cup brandy or rum
1 envelope unflavored gelatin
¼ cup cold water
5 egg yolks, slightly beaten
½ cup sugar
1½ cups milk, scalded
3 egg whites
¼ cup whipping cream, whipped

1. Cut the pound cake into 1-inch pieces. Arrange over bottom of a 2-quart shallow casserole. Pour brandy over cake pieces.

2. Soften gelatin in the cold water. Combine egg yolks with ¼ cup of the sugar in top of a double boiler. Add the scalded milk gradually, blending well. Cook over simmering water, stirring constantly until mixture coats a metal spoon. Immediately remove from heat and stir in gelatin until dissolved. Cool and chill until mixture becomes slightly thicker.

3. Beat the egg whites until frothy; gradually add the remaining ¼ cup sugar, beating constantly until stiff peaks are formed.

4. Spread egg whites and whipped cream over gelatin mixture and gently fold together. Turn into the casserole. Chill until firm.

5. When ready to serve, garnish with **candied cherries, slivered almonds,** and pieces of **angelica.** If desired, garnish with a border of sweetened whipped cream forced through a pastry bag and star decorating tube.

About 12 servings

Walnut Cake

2 cups (about 10 ounces) dark
   seedless raisins
⅔ cup sherry
4 cups sifted all-purpose flour
2 teaspoons baking powder
¼ teaspoon salt
1 teaspoon nutmeg
4 cups (about 1 pound) walnuts
1¼ cups butter or margarine
2 teaspoons grated orange peel
2 cups sugar
6 eggs, well beaten
⅔ cup orange juice
½ cup molasses

1. Lightly grease a 10-inch tube pan. Line bottom with waxed paper cut to fit pan. Lightly grease paper.
2. Put raisins into a bowl. Pour sherry over raisins. Set aside.
3. Sift together flour, baking powder, salt, and nutmeg and set aside.
4. Chop walnuts and set aside.
5. Cream butter and orange peel until softened. Add sugar gradually, creaming until fluffy after each addition.
6. Add eggs gradually, beating thoroughly after each addition. Set aside.
7. Drain raisins, reserving liquid. Mix liquid with orange juice and molasses.
8. Alternately add dry ingredients in fourths and liquid in thirds to creamed mixture, beating only until smooth after each addition. Finally, blend in the raisins and walnuts. Turn batter into pan, spreading evenly to edges.
9. Bake at 275°F 2½ hours, or until cake tests done. Cool completely on cooling rack and remove from pan.

One 10-inch tube cake

Sherried Holiday Pudding

1 package (14 ounces)
   gingerbread mix
¾ cup orange juice
¼ cup sherry
½ cup chopped walnuts
½ teaspoon grated orange peel
Golden Sherry Sauce (see
   recipe)
Hard Sauce Snowballs (see
   recipe)

1. Prepare gingerbread according to package directions using orange juice and sherry for liquid. Add walnuts and orange peel.
2. Turn batter into a well-greased 6-cup mold (batter should fill mold ½ to ⅔ full).
3. Bake at 350°F for 50 to 55 minutes, until pudding tests done. Serve warm with Golden Sherry Sauce and Hard Sauce Snowballs.

8 servings

Golden Sherry Sauce: Combine **½ cup each granulated and brown sugar (packed), ¼ cup whipping cream,** and **⅛ teaspoon salt** in saucepan. Heat slowly to boiling, stirring occasionally. Add **¼ cup sherry** and **1 teaspoon grated lemon peel.** Heat slightly to blend flavors.

About 1⅓ cups sauce

Hard Sauce Snowballs: Beat together **⅔ cup soft butter or margarine, 2 cups confectioners' sugar,** and **1 tablespoon sherry,** adding a little more sherry if more liquid is needed. Shape into small balls and roll in **flaked coconut.**

About 1½ cups or 16 balls

New Orleans Holiday Pudding

3 cups boiling water
1¼ cups prunes
1 cup dried apricots
1 cup sugar
1 teaspoon ground cinnamon
1 teaspoon ground nutmeg

1. Pour boiling water over prunes and apricots in a saucepan. Return to boiling, cover, and simmer about 45 minutes, or until fruit is tender. Drain and reserve 1 cup liquid. Set liquid aside until cold. Remove and discard prune pits.
2. Force prunes and apricots through a food mill or sieve into a large bowl. Stir in a mixture of the sugar, cinnamon, nutmeg,

1 teaspoon ground allspice
1 cup orange juice
3 tablespoons ruby port
3 envelopes unflavored gelatin
1½ cups golden raisins, plumped
2¼ cups candied cherries
⅓ cup diced candied citron
⅓ cup diced candied lemon peel
1½ cups walnuts, coarsely
       chopped
3 envelopes (2 ounces each)
       dessert topping mix, or 3
       cups whipping cream,
       whipped

and allspice, mixing until sugar is dissolved. Blend in orange juice and wine; mix thoroughly.

3. Soften gelatin in the 1 cup reserved liquid in a small saucepan. Stir over low heat until gelatin is dissolved. Stir into fruit-spice mixture. Chill until mixture is slightly thickened, stirring occasionally.

4. Blend raisins, cherries, citron, lemon peel, and walnuts into gelatin mixture.

5. Prepare the dessert topping according to package directions or whip the cream. Gently fold into fruit mixture, blending thoroughly. Turn into 10-inch tube pan. Chill until firm.

6. Unmold onto chilled serving plate.

20 to 24 servings

Sherry Baba Ring

1 package active dry yeast
¼ cup warm water
¼ cup hot milk
½ cup soft butter
3 tablespoons sugar
1 teaspoon salt
4 eggs
2 cups all-purpose flour
   Sherry Syrup
   Whipped cream
   Glacé fruits

1. Soften yeast in water.
2. Combine hot milk, soft butter, sugar, and salt.
3. Beat eggs. Beat in yeast mixture, then butter mixture. Beat in flour thoroughly to make a smooth, thick batter.
4. Turn into a well-buttered 2-quart mold with tube center. Let rise in a warm place until almost doubled in bulk, 1 to 1½ hours.
5. Bake at 375°F for 30 minutes, or until cake tests done. Make sherry syrup while baba is baking.
6. Remove baked baba from oven and allow to cool in pan 10 minutes. Turn baba onto a serving plate. Prick sides and top with tines of a fork. Slowly baste with sherry syrup. Let stand until syrup is almost absorbed.
7. Fill center of ring with slightly sweetened whipped cream and garnish with glacé fruits.

About 8 servings

Sherry Syrup: Simmer **1½ cups sugar** with **⅔ cup water** and **1 tablespoon grated orange peel** 10 minutes. Mix in **½ cup California Cream Sherry** and **¼ cup apricot-pineapple jam.** Simmer 5 minutes; cool.

WINE COOKERY CHART

Foods	Amount	Wines
SOUPS		
Cream soups	1 T per cup	Dry white wine or sherry
Meat and vegetable soups	1 T per cup	Dry red wine or sherry
SAUCES		
Cream sauce	1 T per cup	Sherry or dry white wine
Brown sauce	1 T per cup	Sherry or dry red wine
Tomato sauce	1 T per cup	Sherry or dry red wine
Cheese sauce	1 T per cup	Sherry or dry white wine
Dessert sauce	1 T per cup	Port or muscatel
MEATS		
Pot roast	¼ cup per lb.	Dry red wine
Gravy for roasts	2 T per cup	Burgundy, dry white wine, or sherry
Stew-beef	¼ cup per lb.	Dry red wine
Stew-lamb or veal	¼ cup per lb.	Dry white wine
Ham, baked	2 cups (for basting)	Port or muscatel
Liver, braised	¼ cup per lb.	Burgundy or dry white wine
Tongue, boiled	½ cup per lb.	Dry red wine
FISH		
Broiled, baked or poached	½ cup per lb.	Dry white wine
POULTRY AND GAME		
Chicken	¼ cup per lb.	Dry white wine or red wine
Gravy for roast or fried chicken, turkey	2 T per cup	Dry white or red wine or sherry
Duck, roasted	¼ cup per lb.	Dry red wine
Venison	¼ cup per lb.	Dry red wine
Pheasant	¼ cup per lb.	Dry white or red wine, or sherry
FRUIT (Fresh, canned, or frozen)		
In syrup or juice (fruit cups, compotes, etc.)	2 T per cup *over fruit or in syrup or juice*	Port, muscatel, sherry, rosé, dry white, or red wine
(or) Drained	*At the table, pour over fruits without dilution*	Champagne or other sparkling wines

T = Tablespoon

GLOSSARY

Acidity—The quality of tartness, or sharpness, of a wine. All sound wines contain it. It gives life and charm to the wine. This term should not be confused with dryness, sourness, or astringency.

Apéritif (a-pair′-i-tif)—French word for appetizer; used in connection with wine, it refers to wines served before meals.

Aroma—The fresh, fruity perfume of a newly made wine. This is different from bouquet, which develops with aging.

Astringency—The "puckeriness" of wines, usually derived from tannin from the skins and seeds of grapes. Moderate astringency is considered desirable in red table wines; it lessens with bottle age.

Beaujolais (boh-zhoh-lay′)—A dry, red French wine appropriate for casual dining.

Bouquet—The fragrance that arises from fermentation and aging. Bouquet, especially from an aged wine, can be very complex, and inhaling it gives dimension to the flavor of wine.

Brut (broot)—French term meaning "unmodified." When applied to champagne, it means one to which little or no *dosage* (sweetening) has been added.

Burgundy (bur′-gun-dee)—A French province (Bourgogne) from which come some of the world's best wines: red, white, and some rosé. Chablis, Gamay, Pinot, Chardonnay, Beaujolais, and others come from Burgundy. The name Burgundy has become a generic term for red wine in other parts of the world.

Cabernet (kab-er-nay′)—The red wine grape responsible for the great clarets of Bordeaux.

Cabernet Sauvignon (kab-er-nay′ sew-vee-nyon′) —On a wine label from California, a guide to quality wine. Such wine is said to have a varietal name; this variety produces America's finest clarets.

Chablis (shah-blee′)—A medium dry, white wine. It is one of the most famous of all white Burgundy wines, made from Chardonnay grapes in the Chablis area. The name has become generic and has been applied to other white wines made outside France.

Champagne (sham-pain′)—In France, a sparkling wine made from certain varieties of grapes grown in a limited area near Rheims, east of Paris. The name has been applied to white sparkling wine produced by the champagne process or a variation of it.

Character—Wine experts apply this term to a wine that exhibits in a full degree the qualities of taste, bouquet, and color associated with such a wine at its best.

Chianti (kee-ahn′-tee)—A dry, red Italian wine. An inexpensive version comes in a round-bottomed bottle and goes well with spicy foods such as spaghetti. A more elegant version is Chianti Classico which comes in straight-sided bottles and ages well.

Claret—In England, this term means the red wines of Bordeaux; elsewhere it can mean any red table wine.

Classico—A term applied to Italian wines, such as Chianti and Valpolicella, meaning that the wine comes from the original heartland of a production area.

Clean—A wine giving the effect in the mouth of refreshing purity; swallowed, a sense of cleanliness remains in the mouth and nasal passages.

Cloudy—Wine which has been shaken or poorly fermented can be cloudy. If cloudiness does not disappear with rest, the wine is probably undrinkable.

Coarse—Wine which is rough or lacking in finesse.

Color—This is one of wine's most important characteristics. Color varies from shades of gold and amber through ruby and garnet.

Corked or **corky**—The term "corked wine" is sometimes used for this trait denoting a wine tainted by a defective cork. It imparts a smelly, woody odor to the wine. Corky wines are rare.

Dry—A term to denote lack of sweetness in wine.

Decanting—Pouring wine from its original to another container to separate it from any sediment in the bottom of the bottle. Aged red wines such as Claret and Burgundy often "throw" some sediment and need decanting. This should be done several hours before serving. The bottle is held in a wine cradle, or a "cradle" of folded towel, the cork removed, and wine slowly poured into a decanter. When the sediment begins to appear near bottle neck, pouring should stop.

Dubonnet (dew-boh-nay′)—An aperitif wine usually consisting of a sweet fortified wine with quinine and herbs added.

Flinty—White wines grown in stony soils sometimes have a hard character which the French say is like the smell of flint when struck with steel.

Fortified—A term indicating that the wine has had brandy or other spirits added before bottling to increase alcoholic content.

Fruity—Having the fragrance and flavor of the grape, a freshness, sometimes called "grapey."

Gamay (gam-ay')—Small black-red wine grape from which Beaujolais is made in France. California wines called Gamay and Gamay Beaujolais are made from this grape.

Gewürztraminer (geh-vyurts'-trah-meen'-er)—An Alsatian grape, producing a dry, white wine of a spicy, characteristic aroma. Gewürztraminer wine is produced in France, Germany, and California.

Grape—The fruit of some forty species of the genus *Vitis*, all native to the north temperate zone. *Vitis vinifera* produces most of the world's wine.

Graves (grahv)—Important wine district of Bordeaux, France, producing red wines (clarets) and white. The dry, white Graves is best known in this country.

Grenache Rosé (gren-ahsh' roh-zay')—A dry, pink wine from California.

Grignolino (green-yoh-leen'-oh)—Dry, red table wine from Piedmont, Italy. The grape of this name is widely planted in southern California.

Hock (from Hochheimer)—Term widely used in Great Britain to denote Rhine wines in general.

Kosher wine—A generally sweetened, red wine made under the supervision of a rabbi to conform with Jewish religious laws. It has become popular in the United States and is usually made from Concord grapes.

Lacrima Christi (lah'-kree-ma krees'-ti)—Generally a white wine (sometimes red) grown on the slopes of Mount Vesuvius. A sparkling wine of this name is made in northern Italy.

Lafite-Rothschild (lah-feet' row'-shield)—The name of the chateau producing one of the top-ranking red Bordeaux wines of the Médoc, and one of the world's great clarets.

Lambrusco (lahm-broos'-koh)—Dry, red table wine from Emilia, Italy.

Latour (lah-toor')—Chateau producing one of the top-ranking red Bordeaux wines of the Médoc, and one of the world's great clarets.

Liebfraumilch (leeb'-frow-milsh)—A blended white wine, of no particular vineyard or grape variety. The name means "milk of the Blessed Mother" and was originally given to the wine produced around the Liebfrau Kirche (church) in Worms on the Rhine, and is now applied to almost any Rhine wine.

Light—Not noticeably alcoholic; a refreshing type of wine.

Loire (lwahr)—Wines produced along the valley of this French river are sometimes called Loire wines. They vary, but are mainly white. Best known of the dry white Loire wines are Sancerre, Pouilly, and Muscadet. Much of the wine from the Anjou region is pink.

Madeira (mah-day'-rah)—A whole class of fortified wines which originally came from the Portuguese island of Madeira. These range from very dry (used as aperitif) to very sweet (used as dessert wine).

Marsala (mar-sah'-lah)—An Italian fortified wine, amber in color, which may be either dry or sweet. It originated in Marsala, Sicily, and is often used in recipes.

Mature—A wine that has developed all its characteristic qualities.

Mavrodaphne (mahv-roh-dahf'-nee)—A sweet, red, fortified dessert wine from Greece.

May wine—A semisweet white wine that originated in Germany, but now also produced in California. Often served from a punch bowl with fruit.

Mellow—Soft and luscious, often with some sweetness. Used in reference to some red table wines.

Musty—An odor similar to decaying wood. If found in wine, it should be rejected.

Neuchâtel (new-shah-tell')—A dry, white wine, one of the best known from Switzerland.

Niagara—A semidry white wine from New York State.

Nose—Term for the total fragrance, aroma, and bouquet of a wine.

Orvieto (or-vee-et'-oh)—Wines from the area of the town of Orvieto. Orvieto wine may be dry or sweet, white or pink.

Petillant (pay-tee-yawn)—The French term for a wine which has a slight natural sparkle.

Pinot Blanc (pee-noh blahn')—A dry, white California wine, transplanted from Burgundy, France.

Pinot Chardonnay (pee-no shar-do-nay')—In France, this grape produces all the great white Burgundies, including Chablis, Montrachet, and Pouilly-Fuisse. In California, it produces some of the finest white table wine made in the United States.

Pinot Noir (pee-noh nwahr')—This grape is responsible for all the great red Burgundies, including Pommard, Beaune, Corton, Musigny, and Chambertin. Transplanted in California, this grape produces wine characteristic of its French ancestor.

Pomerol (poh'-mer-all)—A dry, red Bordeaux wine.

Port—Originally from Portugal, this wine is available in white, red, or tawny forms. White port is sometimes served as aperitif; red and tawny for dessert. Authentic port from Portugal is called Porto.

Pouillac (poy-yahk')—A dry, red, Bordeaux wine.

Pouilly-Fuisse (pwee'-yee fwee-say')—A dry, white Burgundy wine.

Pouilly-Fumé (pwee'-yee foo-may')—A dry, white

French wine made from the Sauvignon Blanc or Blanc-Fumé grape.

Rhine wine—German Rhine wine is a dry, white wine from the Rhine Valley. In the United States, any white wine with less than 14 per cent alcohol may use the name. Domestic wines that compare favorably with German Rhine wine are called Johannisberg Riesling and Sylvaner, named for grapes which have been transplanted from Germany.

Rich—A full-bodied wine, well-developed in flavor.

Riesling (rees'-ling)—One of the greatest of white wines; thought to be a native of the Rhine Valley in Germany. It is also cultivated in the Moselle vineyards. In California, wine from this grape is often labeled "Johannisberg Riesling."

Robust—A sturdy, hearty wine, well-developed in flavor and body.

Rosé (roh-zay')—French word for pink; applied to pink wines made anywhere. *Vin rosé* is usually made from black grapes, fermented for two or three days with the skins and husks that impart color, and then drawn off when the desired color is reached.

Sauterne (saw-turn')—A dry to semisweet white wine of California.

Sauternes (soh-tairn)—A sweet wine from Bordeaux, France.

Sec (French) and **secco** (Italian)—Dry, or not sweet.

Sherry—The gold or amber-colored wine originating in the Jerez district of Spain. The word "sherry" is the English pronunciation of *Jerez*. Dry sherry is served as an aperitif; sweet sherry, for dessert. Other countries in addition to Spain produce wine called "sherry"; it is a wine fortified with brandy to around 20 per cent alcohol.

Soave (soh-ah'-veh)—A dry, white Italian wine.

Sound—A term applied to wine that is healthy, pleasant to look at, and good smelling and tasting.

Spritzig (shprit'-sig)—The German equivalent of the French petillant; wine with a slight natural sparkle.

Tart—Possessing agreeable acidity.

Valpolicella (val-pol-lee-cheh'-lah)—A dry, red Italian wine.

Verdicchio (vair-dee'-key-oh)—A dry, white Italian wine.

Vermouth—A dry, white (used in Martinis) or sweet, red (used in Manhattans) appetizer wine. This wine is produced in Italy (the sweet version), France (the dry), and the United States (both).

Vin (van)—French for "wine."

Vino (vee'-no)—Italian for "wine."

Vourvray (voov'-ray)—A semisweet white French wine.

Yquem, Chateau D' (shah-toh dee-kem')—The one Sauternes wine (red or white) to be given the exalted rank of *Grand Premier Cru* in 1855. Probably the most famous vineyard in the world.

Zeller Schwarze Katz (tsel'-er shvahr'-tse kahts')—A dry, white Moselle wine.

Zinfandel (zin'-fan-dell)—A dry, red California grape and wine. It is of the *Vitis vinifera* family, originally from Europe; now not grown extensively anywhere except in California. It is often compared to the Beaujolais of France; a wine best drunk young.

INDEX